# *CLEARMIND*

## The Disentanglement of the Psyche

## Mariano Gallo

CAP
*Publishing*

ISBN-13 (trade paperback): 978-0-9913340-6-3
ISBN-13 (eBook): 978-0-9913340-8-7

Cover image courtesy Shutterstock
Cover design by Bri Bruce Productions

Published by CAP Publishing

*For Antonia, Apollonia, and Cristina*

*"The unexamined life is not worth living."*
—Socrates, at his trial, 399 B.C.

# ACKNOWLEDGMENTS

I deeply appreciate psychologist Linda Harper's help transforming a large pile of words into a book. She served the dual roles of being an on-call clinical advisor and full-time editor-in-chief. Over the course of several years, she provided key insights into the workings of the mind. Her approach provided a calm and steady influence throughout, even when much of the material was difficult to make sense of and weave together. Staying on topic helped avoid missteps, allowing the concepts to come together with a clear focus.

I am grateful for the enormous help of Bri Bruce, designer-publisher-photographer extraordinaire, who was present in all phases of the book's coming to life—its production. She found a way to fit this into her busy schedule. Her feedback brought countless details into focus while working at a quick pace; it was fun keeping up with her. The speed of her efforts matched the skill she continually demonstrated.

And without those brave souls in the old Chicago neighborhoods serving as a reference point, there would be nothing about which to write. They provided a foil, an in-the-trenches, on-the-ground, hard-nosed view of the world, offering gritty insights into the human spirit that I could not have gotten any other way.

Then there are the universities: Loyola, Roosevelt, Northwestern, and Miami, which offered massive amounts of knowledge, as well as financial support. The fellowship the National Institute of Mental Health (NIMH) granted me was a godsend; becoming a psychologist would not have been possible without it. Coursework and one-on-one mentoring helped my understandings of all things clinical. Professors and supervisors gave countless hours of instruction and feedback, clarifying the most critical issues in the field. Clinical work over the years furthered my appreciation for the complexities of the mind.

There were also the creative endeavors of the giants, historical figures in psychology and psychoanalysis whose seminal works still stand. They were the vanguard, providing critical insights into how the mind works. Studying directly with them and those under their tutelage gave me a deeper understanding of their writings.

# CLEARMIND

The Disentanglement of the Psyche

# CONTENTS

## THE ORIGIN OF MIND

## THE STRUCTURE OF PERSONALITY

## THE PROCESS OF THOUGHT

## THE RHYTHM OF LIFE

# PREFACE

Born and raised on the south side of Chicago, I received an early education into the workings of the mind and how individuals think, feel, and act across various conditions. Most people I knew back then had little formal schooling; few graduated high school. Their ability to face the harsh realities of life came from survival instincts and determination. Soundness and practicality weighed heavily on how they saw things. Without fanfare, they spoke what they meant and did what they said they would do.

My experiences and encounters with people in higher educational settings stood in contrast. Universities have a rich history and commitment to teaching and mentoring, gathering and organizing knowledge, and exploring challenging questions across dozens of disciplines. Yet, when it comes to people, they seemed to have missed something of profound significance: *common sense* and its role in understanding behavior and finding practical solutions to problems in living. Theoretical and research-based approaches to the intricate workings of the mind—the hallmark of academic settings—must be tested in life's laboratories.

Coursework and clinical training revealed that the complexities of people's thoughts, feelings, and actions go far beyond any one orientation or even a combination of many. My work in psychology spanning more than four decades supports the conclusion that understanding the mind must be grounded in the realities of everyday life. *Clearmind* represents reconciling the *common sense* approach of ordinary people with the intellectual rigor in psychology.

*Mariano Gallo*
*Chicago, Illinois*
*February 19, 2023*

# INTRODUCTION

In Greek mythology, *Psykhe* is the goddess of the soul, spirit, and mind. The word *psyche* refers to this same essence: the totality of both consciousness and unconsciousness. Striving toward *clearmind* is to disentangle the *psyche*, freeing it from that which binds and unleashing its energies. It can only be a personal endeavor, as people are inherently not the same. *Vive la difference.*

The study of the mind requires a recognition of the extraordinary, breathtaking, spectacular, astonishing, and dazzling uniqueness of the person. It involves paying attention to individual differences in people's thoughts, feelings, and actions rather than overgeneralizing. First and foremost, the person must become aware of oneself before any meaningful change can begin.

*Clearmind*'s attempt is to guide a person toward recognizing the vast nature of one's wondrous, convoluted *psyche*—to look behind the curtain, see its reality, and act on it. The invitation is to use the framework outlined in this book to conceptualize how the mind works, understanding it through these three portals:

1. *An appreciation of conscious and unconscious personality elements that include identity, inner struggles, value system, and inherent tendencies.*

2. *A study of thinking processes that involve intellectual functioning, emotional-cognitive linkages, optimization of thoughts, acute understandings, and the development of approaches to life struggles.*

3. *A review of life patterns that encompass the nuances of identifications and their impact on the personality, stress reactions, continuous mistakes, and challenges in maturation and adaptation.*

By becoming attuned to the *psyche's* functioning, a person can realize and acknowledge who one is and the best ways to get where one is going. The tired, old baggage of self-doubt, uncertainty, and blurred vision is left behind, and in its place is a renewed and invigorated awareness—a clarity of mind.

Central to this pursuit is becoming attentive to everything that enhances understanding oneself and others. But since the mind is in flux, each insight is momentary, merely a clue leading to further investigation. One can only experience *clearmind* as a lifelong process of discovery. How does one begin to understand the definitive components of a fluid mind? Like a kaleidoscope, the mind creates intricate and sophisticated images that change from one multi-dimensional landscape to another with the slightest turn. While a stable view may appear in reach, it is fleeting. Thus, the populist notions of self-image, sense of self, and ego do not accurately reflect the mind's multiple expressions.

Valiant endeavors to explain the comedies and tragedies of human affairs come from divergent sources, including philosophers, theorists, and researchers. While their contributions are vast, this book takes a different approach to "what makes people tick." It is one clinical psychologist's perspective on the disentangling of the *psyche*. *Clearmind* offers a framework upon which philosophical treatises, personality theories, scientific research, and life experiences may rest while recognizing each mind's uniqueness and ever-changing nature.

# FOUNDATIONS OF CLEARMIND

High in the sky, an eagle in flight has a breathtaking panorama of the world below. Similarly, an overview of the conceptual underpinnings of *Clearmind* will hopefully prove helpful in understanding the mind. The basic framework of the book's central tenants are as follows:

*Personal Identity (PI)*. The concept of identity is multi-faceted; it is more complex, tangled, and elaborate than one can imagine. Identity involves several overlapping and interconnecting dimensions, the most fundamental being *personal identity (PI)*, the sense of who the person is. It consists of those distinct qualities and character features that a person has come to embrace, consciously and unconsciously, which distinguishes one person from another.

*Interpersonal Identity (II)*. How a person sees and defines oneself through one-on-one contacts and communications make up *interpersonal identity (II)*. One's interactions with people across the spectrum of situations and circumstances reverberate throughout the personality, powerfully impacting the specific attributes of this identity.

*Collective Identity (CI)*. A person's connections to groups – including associations, institutions, and even ideas about them – create the *collective identity (CI)*. Common influences of group identification include familial experiences, school involvements, ethnic and racial backgrounds, community and culture, work, political interests, military service, and religious commitments.

**The Transpersonal Identity (TI)**. One cannot completely know the basis of *transpersonal identity (TI)* because it comes from a mystical belief in a non-material, non-quantifiable reality. It is not the product of logical analysis but primarily relies on faith and spiritual intuition. Influencing experiences include wondrous moments that may cause a person to redefine himself.

**Pathos.** The *personal identity's* evil twin consists of emotionally charged aspects of the person that cause an expansion of negative images toward oneself and others. Of all the factors that make up the personality, *pathos* is the embodiment and primary measure of psychological dysfunction. It is an outgrowth of *PI* and presents as an extension and exaggeration. A lack of love, affection, warmth, structure, and acceptance in childhood can create a complex of adversarial, hurting, and hurtful traits. *Pathos* develops throughout one's life from conflicts, traumas, malevolent identifications (CTMI), and emotionalism, defined as follows:

- *Conflicts.* Disagreements within oneself or with others that create an internal struggle over issues involving aggression, assertiveness, intimacy, achievement, ambition, trust, or independence. When blocked from consciousness, they recede into the background.

- *Traumas.* Distressing and disturbing experiences that may emotionally exhaust a person and continue to cause psychological dysfunction on both conscious and unconscious levels.

- *Malevolent identifications.* Powerful and intense connections to a person, institution, or idea leading to unprincipled, inhumane, or maladaptive thoughts, feelings, and actions (TFA). An attraction to particular qualities—even if they are bizarre and destructive—leads to their creation.

- *Emotionalism.* Extreme emotional responses creating a pattern of overreactions beyond what societal norms consider reasonable or appropriate. It is a chronic condition, including rage, deep depression, severe panic, debilitating anxiety, and para-

6

lyzing fear that may dominate a person's life.

**Directives.** The factors that make up a person's *directives* (value system) include motivations, desires, wants, and needs. Goals, dreams, plans, and schemes may be included. Values result from identifications with another person, institution, organization, image, or idea. *Directives* affect all aspects of TFA but can cause inconsistency in one's everyday behavior when idealized and abstract. They do not hold "equal status" for a person; some have greater significance than others. When some values receive significantly more attention than others, *directives* can be out of balance, and obsessions, compulsions, and addictions (OCA) may become dominant.

**Spiritus.** The motivating force within every human being—in fact, within every living creature—is the breath of life. It is one's essence, a *sine qua non*, the inherent guiding principle from which thoughts, feelings, and actions emerge. *Spiritus* consists of innate, distinct, and unique qualities and represents the innermost nature and disposition of the person. The origins of *spiritus* are unknown, but it is not the result of early life experiences, early learning opportunities, or classical conditioning, nor is it the product of CTMI.

**The Process of Thought.** Thinking processes require a person to be alert and conscious of one's world, accurately perceiving what is there and comprehending its meaning and significance. Cognitive functions of the intellect include mental drive, initial listening, sustained attention, memory, logical thought, objectification or realism, practical reasoning, coherence, organization, simplification, attention to detail, intuition, openness to experience, perception, multidimensional thinking, inspired and original thought, and vision. These thinking processes are not separate and distinct; many require several cognitions to work together simultaneously.

The Origin of Mind

# I.
# BEGINNINGS & BEYOND

When wildflowers begin to sprout, one wonders what will be forthcoming. Initially indistinguishable from the other plant life, their nature becomes apparent only when the minerals of the earth, the warmth of the sun, and the nutrients of rainfall bring them forth. Similarly, people's characteristics and qualities only develop and become evident over time and through life experiences.

## Early Experiences

The child's instinctual and emotional reactions to the parents play a critical role in the mind's development. These first years of life are a prelude to mind, allowing for its expansion if and when a support system is in place.

Books on the maturation process of children are plentiful, offering different theories and focuses. Despite their contrasting orientations, some commonalities exist with general agreement on several points: when a child's home environment is stable, loving, and nurturing, with reasonable rules, development continues at a steady pace. Conversely, when the home's atmosphere is chaotic, cold, or hostile, the child's psychological growth will be negatively affected. It may not be quite that simple, but overall these generalizations hold across cultures and civilizations. While one cannot say with certainty which parenting styles will lead to a well-adjusted child, the following factors positively affect the developmental process:

- *Emotional stability.* A cohesive family setting that provides a sense of security and safety.

- *Nurturance.* Care and provision for the children. The family setting is emotionally supportive and encouraging without pampering, spoiling, or overindulging. Support provides a reasonable degree of structure to the child's pursuits while allowing for independent action.

- *Rules and expectations.* Appropriate limits set. The parents state clear guidelines and reinforce them consistently and fairly.

- *Teachings.* Family history that includes stories, folklore, and traditions.

- *Validation.* Providing affirmations without an exaggeration or distortion of children's achievements.

- *Warmth.* An emotional state that radiates friendliness, closeness, familiarity, and intimacy. Similar to nurturance, warmth allows the children to develop with a sense of acceptance and value.

- *Modeling of maturity.* Positive qualities displayed by the parents. Reliability and compassion promote emotional development.

- *Communications.* Positive verbal and nonverbal interactions. In addition to direct expression of thoughts, feelings, and actions (TFA), messages to the child occur through body language, tone of voice, and facial expression. Children learn to speak directly and respectfully to their parents when the subtleties of parent-child communication are consistent in words and deeds.

## Disciplining the Child

What are the lasting effects of parental discipline on the developing child? Some approaches are positive and productive, providing structure and guidance, while others are destructive and harmful.

Although the exact ways mistreatment will influence a person's TFA are individually determined and unpredictable, the impact will be negative on many levels, with all elements of the personality adversely affected. While harsh punishments may immediately suppress certain behaviors, they have long-term negative implications, including rage reactions, debilitating anxieties, uncontrolled panic attacks, significant mood disorders, or obsessive worrying. Furthermore, a child may strongly identify with a punishing parent and adopt the same negative traits.

## Stress Experienced During Childhood

One's development will be impaired if subjected to repeated stress during childhood. Although these experiences may not rise to the level of traumatic events, their early occurrences can impact the personality for the following reasons:

- *Consciousness.* Many adverse experiences in the childhood years remain primarily unconscious. Compared to an adult, emotional stability and cognitive capacity are largely undeveloped, rendering a child unable to understand or process these experiences at a conscious level.

- *Layers and layers of living life.* Emotional reactions vary in significance and intensity and may lay buried under multiple years of stressful life events. Their sheer volume makes those experiences difficult to retrieve and bring into consciousness.

- *The identification process.* Positive emotional connections formed during childhood are crucial to developing a stable and consistent identity.

**Beyond the Childhood Years**

Human development does not follow stages that strictly conform to specific timelines. Development springs forth when needs are met, wants are satisfied, and instincts are understood and trusted. Multiple layers of identifications, conflicts, and learning opportunities—as well as mundane life experiences—flow through one's essence and create a multidimensional personality. These early identifications and experiences form the foundation of the personality, serving as the necessary forerunners for the development of a person.

**Needs**

Inherited physiology and a unique genetic blueprint play significant roles in human needs, but psychological and habitual forces also potently influence a person's thoughts, feelings, and actions (TFA). The three basic types of needs are physiological, psychological, and acquired, defined as follows:

- *Physiological needs.* Required to sustain life and physically survive. Food, water, air, shelter, and climatic conditions are all examples of basic biological needs.

- *Psychological needs.* Not only contact with people but also with other living things. Additionally, intellectual and physical stimulation are essential. Deprivation of psychological needs affects one's ability to think, analyze, understand, and draw proper conclusions; anxiety, depression, and anger may also increase.

- *Acquired needs.* Repetitive behaviors reinforced by the momentary reduction of stress. Addictions are the most common form of problematic acquired needs and include repetitive behavioral patterns that negatively impact a person's life. Examples include alcoholism and drug abuse, excessive eating rituals, nonstop gaming, out-of-control gambling, and sexual preoccupations. Wants can morph into acquired needs, and problems compound when several cravings are involved. Without realizing that these compulsions have become as powerful as the need to sustain life, the person's life spins out of control, needing a "fix" to function.

## Wants

In addition to needs, wants play an essential role in one's life choices. Preferences become more defined as a person develops and forms a rough draft of one's value system. Wants will vary from mild attractions to full-blown cravings. Spending time with family and friends, attending a concert, eating a pizza, and gaining acceptance to a college are all examples of wants. When they expand and evolve into acquired needs, a person becomes controlled by them.

## Instincts

Instincts are part of a person's animal heritage and connection to the natural world. They can provide an intuitive understanding that helps one make decisions at critical moments. Although instincts are not always correct, they may give a person an advantage; they are subliminal, visual, and visceral. They offer an impression about people, situations, and circumstances (PSC) on a level beyond logic or deductive reasoning. They may, however, also be unsound and unwise. Poor decisions may result when a person only listens to instincts without considering these implications and potential negative consequences. The extent to which instincts play a role in one's life will significantly vary from person to person. Some individuals are greatly influenced by these urges, while others are only minimally. Instinctual reactions vary in their strength, quality, and etiology, affecting TFA in the following ways:

- *Intuitive understanding.* An awareness that is useful, fitting, and appropriate flows effortlessly to guide the person in understanding the issues one is facing.

- *Unconscious determinants.* Thought patterns emerge and influence behavior but are not part of deliberate, calculated decision-making.

- *Innate impressions or inklings.* Although one cannot explain the reason for certain feelings, reactions occur instantaneously in response to PSC. Examples include taking an immediate liking or disliking to a person or having highly positive or negative thoughts and feelings about a situation or circumstance. These responses are unrelated to drives for survival, nourishment, sex, aggression, nurturance, and physical closeness and are not the result of formal education, analysis, or planning.

# CHAPTER I QUESTIONS

1.  What childhood experiences do you vividly recall?

2.  What did you find particularly stressful in childhood?

3.  Were your psychological needs met growing up?

4.  Have acquired needs been problematic?

5.  What are your wants, and how do they impact your choices?

6.  Do instincts play a role in your decision-making? How?

# II.

# THE IDENTIFICATION PROCESS

In the 18th Century, the Amish people of Lancaster County, Pennsylvania, engaged in "barn-raising," building barns for families in their community. The labor and lumber would bind them together as they celebrated their connection to one another. Every aspect of this shared experience becomes a part of the identification process that defines who and what one is, affecting the entire personality—personal growth, behaviors, attitudes, and values. This process is not simple or straightforward but complicated and enigmatic because it requires the blending together of four forms: *personal identity (PI), interpersonal identity (II), collective identity (CI),* and *transpersonal identity (TI).*

### Deliberate and Nondeliberate Self-Descriptions

Relationships with parental figures are the cornerstone of a person's first identifications. Initially formed by preverbal unconscious images, these observations and experiences significantly impact the creation of *personal identity (PI).* In early childhood, one has not yet developed critical thinking; raw feelings, instincts, impulses, and *spiritus* are the primary influences of these first years of life.

Understanding the identification process requires recognizing the roles of the three entwined states of awareness—the conscious, semi-conscious, and unconscious (see Chapter VI, States of Awareness). The sea of consciousness is murky water; where does one form of awareness leave off and the other begin? A person is fully aware of conscious thoughts and images; they are deliberate, calculated, intentional, and purposeful. This level of awareness seems to come and go, but overall, the person is alert to what is going on. Conscious thought processes include logical thinking, talking, listening, focused attention, imagining, planning, and analyzing. But many forms of identification are not deliberate choices. Unconscious identifications may contradict conscious ones and result in a person subscribing to a particular set of beliefs about oneself while appearing to live by an entirely different standard. Thus, identifications can be paradoxical and contradictory, as when a person checks boxes on a self-report that do not reflect one's behavior.

The four forms of identification commonly work with varying degrees of disagreement. For example, a person's *PI* may exude peace and harmony, while one's *CI* identifies with aggressive, perhaps even violent groups. At the same time, the *TI* connects to God, whom is perceived as merciful and forgiving. A person may appear to be a walking contradiction, with actions reflecting the four forms of identification expressing themselves in particular ways.

### The Role of Emotions in the Identification Process

Whether overly expressed or covertly experienced, emotions play a critical role in the identification process and, by extension, in creating the personality. They are often the conscious or unconscious responses to a perceived change in a person's life. Although identifications usually have a cognitive component, they tend to be primal and elemental because they are the product of associations or a person's attempt to copy what one sees. An emotional part always fuels an identification's formation, giving it force, passion, energy, and endurance.

The strength rather than the type of emotion has a greater impact. The more intense the feeling—as experienced with anger, hurt, abandonment, grief, passion, admiration, and love—the more powerful the identifications will be. The following types of emotions affect the identification process:

- *Raw emotions.* An entirely visceral expression of emotions with little or no cognitive component.

- *Emotional memories.* To vividly recall events in one's life and intensely reexperience the emotional component.

- *Emotions that surround the person's PI, II, CI, and TI.* The distinct and definitive characteristics of intrapsychic, interpersonal, group, and spiritual experiences, each with a particular emotional resonance.

## Principles in the Identification Process

Identifications shape the view of oneself, other people, and the world; they directly influence a person's construct of reality and understanding of one's surroundings. The following principles apply to the formation of an identity:

- *Over-Identifying.* When overly attached to another person, institution, or even an idea, one will lock into that association and disregard other possible influences.

- *Consciousness.* When identifications are unconscious or semiconscious, a person will have less control over thoughts, feelings, and actions.

- *Multiple and diversified identifications.* Contradictions will likely result when *PI, II, CI,* and *TI* significantly differ. A person may create numerous identities through work history, habits and hobbies, political philosophies, religious affiliations and faith, community and culture, family and friends, alliances and commitments. What draws a person to these kinds of specific identifications? Possibilities include experiencing a sense of power, peace, belonging, closeness, security, purpose, and religious devotion. But when multiple identifications are simply random impressions, a person forms a patchwork of an identity. *PI, II, CI,* and *TI* may not be in sync with the other personality elements; disharmony and dispute among the forms of identification are likely to occur, causing conflict and friction across the entire personality structure.

- *Substance vs. style.* Identifications tend to be along different dimensions, with varying levels of significance for a person. Some rest on substance and are based on meaningful principles, while others form because of style, focusing on the surface characteristics of someone or something. Inevitably, subjectivity will enter into one's perspective because what one person views as substance, another will see as style.

- *Triggers.* A person's identity can suddenly appear to change, set off by people, situations, or circumstances (PSC). The exact causes for this abrupt alteration of the person's identity can be challenging to pinpoint; it may result from a singular influence or a chain of events.

- *Imagery vs. logic.* While logical analysis and step-by-step conceptualizations have their place, connections often come from images, impressions, and emotional associations.

- *Sensitivities and vulnerabilities.* One's perceived degree of acceptance or rejection strongly influences identification. The subtleties of these interactions—body language, tone and volume of voice, facial expression, hesitations and pauses, interruptions, firmness in the way one speaks, and movements of the hands and arms—play a role in experiences and intensify in face-to-face interactions. While less obvious and seemingly insignificant, these nonverbal communications can profoundly affect the identifications one is drawn to, especially when repeated.

- *Endurance.* A lasting identification will form when a person reacts to physical or emotional hurt. Under these conditions, a person may assume similar or opposing personality traits of the one who caused the hurting, both on conscious or unconscious levels. For example, one could identify with someone abusive and intolerant and take on those characteristics, although outwardly display disdain. Then again, one may develop a nurturing and tolerant disposition when exposed to painful PSC. A further illustration of the complexity of the identification process is a person with great admiration for a saint but not the slightest inclination to adopt any of those attributes.

# CHAPTER II QUESTIONS

1. Who were the strongest influences in your early years?

2. How have people, relationships, group involvements, and spiritual connections affected your life?

3. Do these influences seem to agree with one another, or are they continually in conflict?

4. Are these connections more in the head or the heart?

5. How do the emotional connections, in particular, impact how you see yourself?

6. Are you generally aware of their influences on you, or are some just happening?

7. What aspects of yourself seem contradictory and difficult to understand?

# III.

# THE ENVIRONMENTAL PRESS: PEOPLE, SITUATIONS, AND CIRCUMSTANCES

On April 14, 1935, one of the worst storms in the history of the United States hit parts of New Mexico, Oklahoma, Kansas, Colorado, and the Texas Panhandle. The day became known as Black Sunday when dust from 100 mph winds blanketed over a thousand miles of the Great Plains, devastating farms and communities. But the human spirit prevailed during the "Dust Bowl." People adapted, adjusted, survived, and persevered.

The mind also faces its own challenges; it doesn't exist in a vacuum. Understanding the multifaceted influences of life experiences on the mind allows one to learn and profit from them. A person makes continual adjustments when encountering the outer world of people, situations, and circumstances (PSC), coming face to face with the good, the bad, and the ugly on a daily basis.

## Defining People, Situations, and Circumstances

The forces in the world that one encounters and embraces—people, situations, and circumstances—are defined as follows:

- *People.* Unlimited types of interactions with others that can be fleeting or continuous, straightforward or complex, peaceful or argumentative, loving or hateful. These exchanges strongly influence human identifications.

- *Situations.* A somewhat predictable and planned set of events in which a person typically has an opportunity to prepare a response. Examples of situations involve routine activities such as going to school or work, getting together with family or friends, playing a game of golf, or preparing dinner.

- *Circumstances.* Unexpected, unplanned, abrupt, and unforeseen events occurring when a person is already in a given situation. Circumstances are unpredictable and do not follow the ordinary, routine course of affairs. The suddenness of these events allows for little time to prepare a response.

In addition to developing an appreciation for the complexities of people, one learns to distinguish between situations and circumstances. For example, a person owns and operates a small bakery. Then, out of nowhere, devastating storms come through the area and damage the shop. The running of the business is a situation, and the storms are a circumstance. Another example is a doctoral candidate with a completed dissertation preparing for its defense. The student knows that some committee members may be problematic, but has confidence that the chair can "keep them in line." Then the unthinkable happens: the chair passes away days before the defense, and a new one is needed. The painstaking work on the dissertation and the up-and-coming defense represent the situation, and the dead chair is the circumstance.

In these two examples, the situations are life proceeding in a challenging but mostly predictable way. The circumstances, however, disrupt the expected flow, and suddenly, the intended outcomes become uncertain. But circumstances do not always imply dreadful conditions; they can include pleasant experiences such as a surprise birthday party, a job promotion, or inheriting a  desperately needed sum of money.


### The Environmental Press and the Personality

The ways the environmental press influence people vary widely because of individual differences. Both external and internal factors influence each person's thoughts, feelings, and actions. For example, the degree to which someone's unkind words hurt one's feelings differs from person to person; the insult and the particulars of the individual receiving it determine the response. So although personality is a primary determinant in one's perception of PSC, the particular environmental press must be considered an objective component of the interaction.

## The Forming of Associations with People, Situations, and Circumstances

All people have vulnerabilities that cause them to elicit highly specific responses to what is "out there," the environmental press. Cathexis—the depth of the emotional connection to the particulars of PSC—determines the strength of the associations; strong links cause a person to react in specific ways. This emotional energy fuels the linkage and allows it to occur. The energy source can be any emotion: love, warmth, coldness, acceptance, rejection, infatuation, joy, enthusiasm, excitement, fear, disgust, affection, loathing, anger, meanness, callousness, anxiety, etc. In general, the stronger the emotion, the stronger the cathexis.

When first exposed to a PSC, a person establishes a lasting connection; it is a way of seeing, experiencing, or thinking that may be conscious or unconscious. The original PSC have a particular emotional charge (cathexis) associated with them that transfers to a similar PSC. The linkages cause the person to respond to person B as if person A, situation B as if it were situation A, or circumstance B as if it were circumstance A. The conditioning process occurs when a person forms associations to PSC, creating a generalization that results in a biased viewpoint. Frequently, this prejudgment will result in false ideas about PSC.

Because of these tendencies and vulnerabilities, PSC similar to the original conditions tend to continually reinforce the emotional connection or cathexis. The responses to these PSC form quickly and become ingrained with repeated exposure to similar ones. The experience is self-reinforcing—although it may not be enriching or enjoyable—because it confirms what the person "knows to be true," providing a measure of consistency, stability, and satisfaction.

## The Role of Personality

Personality characteristics that help a person maneuver through the complexities and contradictions of PSC include being:

- *Assertive.* Displaying confidence and leadership in one's positions and interactions.

- *Dispassionate, calm, and composed.* Not overreacting, even under highly stressful conditions.

- *Present.* Keeping one's focus and remaining aware of what is going on, regardless of the extent of the challenge.

- *Impartial and objective.* To retain the capacity to reason and put aside emotionalism and potential bias.

- *Balanced.* Having identity and values in harmony.

- *Committed to understanding.* Demonstrating self-discipline to know both the details and conceptual underpinnings of problem areas.

- *Plain and unassuming.* Acting in a straightforward manner rather than making things overly complicated or confusing.

Personality characteristics that impede fruitful interactions with PSC include being:

- *Low in energy.* Displaying a lack of initiative and letting things "just happen" with a *que sera, sera* approach to problem-solving.

- *Passive-aggressive.* Showing resentment and hostility indirectly, finding a way to blame others for problems.

- *Non-conforming and rebellious.* Doing one's "own thing" and going against the grain by being obstinate and resistant to change. When a person does not enjoy working with others, anything and everything can result in an argument. It takes very little to offend, even infuriate, with loud and forceful intimidation tactics often utilized.

- *Immature.* Not readily accepting responsibilities or following through with assignments, or not acting reasonably and reliably.

- *Socially unskilled.* Acting inappropriately with deficiencies in interpersonal abilities.

- *Overcontrolling, obsessive, perfectionistic.* Emphasizing rules and procedures while giving unimportant details too much weight, and missing relevant information and issues. Insecurity is present, causing rigidity, stubbornness, and intolerance; cooperation and compromise are lacking.

- *Aggressive and hyper-competitive.* Dominating and perhaps humiliating others. Hostile tendencies are valued over productivity and achievement. When the person is in a position of authority, others' lives are made difficult.

- *Political and manipulative, deceptive, controlling, calculating, and scheming.* Lacking integrity and utilizing underhanded tactics to exploit others.

## The Role of Cognition

Beyond the role of the personality, applying different approaches helps a person understand PSC. A person may use all these methods at one time or another, primarily just one or two of them, or none in attempting to resolve problems encountered with PSC, including:

- *Conceptual.* A holistic or big-picture understanding of PSC under study. One develops insights by looking for the guiding principles that underlie PSC.

- *Data-gathering.* To collect as much information as possible, and then as if working on a puzzle, put the accumulated data in place to form a picture. This approach is empirical and dedicated to understanding the details of PSC.

- *Organizational.* A step-by-step, procedural approach to problem-solving. Methods include anticipation and planning, and the development of strategies and fallbacks.

- *Analytic.* The straightforward use of logic. It utilizes deductive reasoning alone in contrast to the conceptual approach that relies on a holistic template.

- *Instinctual.* To look at things without preconceived notions of what is to come next. It is an impromptu, lets-not-get-too-ahead-of-ourselves approach; the person goes with an intuitive hunch primarily based on experiential knowledge and awareness.

- *Empathetic.* Utilizes specific ways of categorizing based on an affinity and connection with a person, institution, or even an idea. They guide in helping make distinctions among all that one encounters.

### The Role of Cognitive-Personality Interactions

When the elements of personality and cognitions combine harmoniously (see Chapter XVI, Cognitive-Personality Connections), they increase a person's ability to focus by enhancing the following skills:

- *Listening.* To put aside distractions, preoccupations, worries, and disappointments so one can attune to the subtleties of PSC.

- *Staying on track.* To remain focused on the task at hand, not allowing extraneous TFA to take root helps provide clarity even when PSC have the following qualities:

  > *Confusion.* PSC can lack organization. Things don't seem to make sense. One needs to look for the central message.

  > *Complications.* Complications differ from confusion in that one's understanding of PSC makes sense, but many variables do not seem to go together as expected. The amount of information available may be excessive, preventing it from connecting in a meaningful way. A careful sorting through of materials is required to achieve clarity.

  > *Complexities.* Sometimes, PSC are challenging to understand because they involve intricate and sophisticated factors. While they may not be disorganized or have excessive details, the content is intrinsically problematic and multifaceted. One may need to find ways to simplify the materials.

- *Resisting being drawn in by an initial appeal.* Whatever it is that initially attracts a person will be a determining factor in the ways in which the PSC are seen, for good or ill. PSC may be dismissed on an immediate feeling, sensation, or quick impression rather than merit. Furthermore, if a person's values are at odds with PSC, one may be less able to use objective analysis to understand them. However, if values are similar, the person may also lose one's impartiality having become captivated by an attraction that brings sentiment or fantasy.

- *Becoming aware of bias and prejudging.* The underlying influ-

ences of the personal agendas of others can affect one's perception and understanding of PSC when one is taken in by
cleverly worded phrases and images. Knowing what is going
on requires awareness of one's personality makeup. Only when
understanding one's own vulnerabilities will a person be able
to comprehend the motivations of others.

# CHAPTER III QUESTIONS

1. What are your interactions with people like, at their best and their worst?

2. Are you able to deal effectively with life's routines?

3. How do you handle unexpected happenings?

4. What personal characteristics help or hinder your ability to deal with PSC?

5. How do you think through a problem?

6. How do you rate your listening skills?

7. Can you stay focused on the task at hand?

8. Are you quickly drawn in by an initial appeal?

9. What preconceived notions do you have about PSC?

# IV.
# THOUGHTS

A penny for your thoughts? That's all they are worth if the elements that define one's state of mind are not working in harmony. Thinking requires the brain, but thoughts are more than the interplay of neurological connections; they are a conglomerate of cognitions, feelings, impressions, and the belief system a person adopts. The continual interactions of these influences create the process of thought. Only through their integration and alignment can one sort through the randomness and unproductiveness of thinking operations, allowing problem-solving through learning, musing, and reflecting.

**The Interplay Between Thoughts, Feelings, and Actions**

Understanding the process of thinking can only begin with recognizing the interconnectedness of thoughts, feelings, and actions (TFA) in response to people, situations, and circumstances (PSC). Because thinking and feeling are intertwined, it is difficult to determine where thoughts leave off and emotions begin. Sometimes thinking precedes an emotional response; a person works oneself into a frenzy by repeatedly going over something that has happened. Other times the emotional response comes first; a person is taken off guard by unsettling news, only to later ponder what has occurred. Thoughts and feelings may lead one to act or hold back. But when all are in sync, one can usually observe the ways they connect. These TFA, individually or in combination, impact a person's development of traits, states, and perspectives as follows:

- *Traits.* One's experiences in living a life—the story, the entire personality, and the chronicity of conflicts, traumas, and malevolent identifications (CTMI)—create enduring traits. They involve the repetition of a particular set of thoughts, feelings, or actions. Examples include being aggressive, silly, obnoxious, or serious. They are a person's consistent and lasting qualities; TFA sometimes reflect them, but other times are merely random or insignificant occurrences. Possessing a certain trait does not mean that a person will consistently demonstrate it because, depending on the PSC involved, an aversive consequence may occur if one reveals it. That trait, however, still exists in thoughts and feelings even when the person's actions do not show it; censoring or editing (see Chapter XIII, Directives) can disguise underlying intentions. An example is a person who is chronically angry but submissive and subdued in meetings with the boss; inner thoughts and feelings reveal one's actual trait.

- *States.* A relatively temporary condition, usually causing fatigue and dysfunction due to sleep deprivation, alcohol intoxication, drug ingestion, acute or long-standing health problems, or brief but intense emotional reactions that can energize or deplete a person.

- *Perspectives.* A person's overarching view reflects one's personality elements, whether or not integrated and balanced. A person's conceptualization of PSC may affect one's reactions in the following ways:

  > *Bias.* Repetitively experienced emotions can affect a person's TFA. For example, if a person continually views reality through a negative emotional lens, this pessimistic outlook will affect one's usual response. Likewise, repeated thoughts can impact emotions and actions; a person may talk oneself into being angry. The following influencing factors can result in a biased response:

    o *Attitude.* A preconceived mindset affects the emotional response. For example, a person with opinions set in stone may become easily agitated, affecting one's decision-making abilities. However, a person with a positive attitude may be open to and tolerant of diverse opinions.

    o  *Expectations.* A strong belief that an event will have a particular outcome can cause a person to become angry or depressed when things don't go as expected. One may become "psyched out" and experience excessive anxiety over falling short of a goal. Patience, tolerance, and realistic views can temper this tendency to cast judgments. A person's belief that things will go well can positively impact oneself and others, resulting in optimism and enthusiasm about projected outcomes.

   ➤  *Street smarts.* Deficiencies in common sense and sharpness affect one's ability to interpret PSC accurately. A misreading of intentions or unwarranted suspicion results in misinterpretations.

## Thought-Emotion Connections

Thoughts can cause emotions, and emotions can cause thoughts; these instantaneous and automatic connections are influenced by:

- *Internal thoughts.* The thoughts alone, positive or negative, that can sometimes trigger the same emotional response as an environmental press. For example, simply thinking about a past confrontation with the boss may be upsetting, just as remembering a summer day at an amusement park with friends can be uplifting.

- *Incidental emotional gain.* An indirect, accidental, and unintentional response that results in a benefit. For example, a person's behaviors may cause sympathy, giving one extra time off work; or someone grieving or experiencing other emotional pain could elicit an empathetic response from a stranger. These gains occur in tandem with a person's actions, not from a strategy or plan. Thus, conditioning occurs through the reinforcement of an emotional response, even though there was no deliberate attempt to profit from it.

• *Intentional emotional gain.* The direct and deliberate manipulation of PSC to take advantage of another to benefit oneself. For example, a person may intentionally overreact to get one's way.

**Thought Without Personality and Emotional Connections**

Pure thought—without emotions and personality entering in—is theoretically possible, but to what degree? Mathematics, the natural sciences, and some branches of philosophy value this type of thinking. Still, even these thought processes fall short of being completely void of emotional connections. Because PSC and the elements of personality continually impact the mind, thinking will be affected. Chapter XVI, Cognitive-Personality Connections, addresses these issues in depth.

**Mind Cluttering**

When the mind becomes "cluttered" with a multitude of thoughts, regrets, and concerns, cognitive processing is not optimal. When bogged down with endless possibilities, a person is unable to make clear decisions. While these thoughts may initially be the product of reasoning, they may spin out of control, becoming torturous, long-standing, and resistant to change. Although the mind can become cluttered in many ways, the most common examples of these experiences are as follows:

- *Feelings of failure.* Repetitive self-blaming occurs even if a person did nothing wrong.

- *Guilt.* A person may experience remorse over actions or lack thereof. While it may be reasonable to feel responsible for what has occurred, one can become overwhelmed with guilt that affects emotional, intellectual, and physical well-being.

- *Regret based on lost opportunity.* A person may continuously think about "what could have been" if only one had followed through when given the chance. Perhaps fear stopped the person, or maybe it didn't seem like a good idea at that time. Whatever the reason, one took a pass and now regrets it.

- *Disappointment.* A person may feel distressed about the way that one handled PSC; one didn't perform perfectly. The memory of something that did not go exactly as planned continually reappears.

- *Grieving.* Having sad feelings due to the loss of a person or a beloved pet is a normal response. But unrelenting painful repetitive thoughts about the loss can impede healing and debilitate a person's functioning.

- *Disillusionment based on a loss of status.* A person perceives that a standing, position, or role in life is diminishing. One has experienced a loss in a critically important area of life; job, marriage, financial security, or home may be in doubt.

- *Ruminating.* When a person has developed a thought process that involves chronic worrying, one obsesses over anything and everything. A characteristic feature of this thinking pattern includes "what could go wrong?" The person can become increasingly pessimistic, with obsessive thoughts reinforcing preoccupations. Thought patterns can become ingrained and affect a person's overall sense of well-being.

- *Vindictive.* When a person believes one "has been wronged," and obsesses on getting even—the vendetta. The thoughts of revenge can increase in frequency and bitterness, possibly resulting in acting out against the person or institution held responsible for the misfortune.

## Problematic Cognitions

Consciously and unconsciously, a person develops ways to deal with people, situations, and circumstances (see Chapter XIX, Strategic Philosophy). Cognitive approaches that are ineffective and can become harmful and destructive include:

- *Inhibitions.* A type of emotional paralysis in TFA, with the person unable to move beyond a gripping fear. One cannot break free from doubt and dread when this fear becomes longstanding.

- *Internalization.* Not recognizing and addressing TFA (see Chapter XIII, Directives) resulting in the partial and temporary dismissing of psychologically painful states. While these tactics may give some relief, the issues remain unresolved and continue to affect the person on an unconscious level. Furthermore, blocking, editing, and censoring effects are not limited to hiding unpleasant TFA but can also cause a diminishing awareness of everyday experiences.

- *Displacement.* An indirect expression of TFA toward someone or something unrelated or tangentially related to the original provocation or cause. Not having dealt with the relevant issues, the person has not resolved the actual problems.

- *Perseveration.* The recycling of TFA. Perseveration in words and images, followed by strong emotional reactions, can quickly become persistent and deep-rooted because the thought process reinforces the emotional response even without external stimuli. For example, a person feels slighted by a previous encounter with someone and angrily obsesses and ruminates over it. Or one may become enthralled and consumed with a new relationship, continually reviewing, replaying, and experiencing it.

## The Influence of the Unconscious on Thoughts, Feelings, and Actions

Past interactions and memories can continue to impact a person's current TFA because, consciously and unconsciously, these experiences are interacting and bound together. Present-day TFA, however, do not *necessarily* have to do with past experiences, and they may not reveal a linkage. Even if a historical context *appears* to be present, a *causal* connection between past experiences and current behaviors may not be proven. Current TFA—including severely pathological and even bizarre behavioral patterns—may have nothing to do with links to the past. While a person cannot fully know the origins of one's TFA, attempting to sort out issues from the past is still vital.

In summary, two possibilities regarding the potential effects of early experiences include:

- *Current behaviors result from present-day experiences and are entirely divorced from the past.* Although CTMI from the past may have sent one down a particular path, no active connection currently influences the person. Even if a cause-effect association existed at one time, if that linkage is no longer present, it is now not relevant.

- *An unconscious nexus may form, mainly when there has been a blockage of cognitive-emotional connections.* If a person's experiences are not recognized and resolved, they may continue to affect perceptions, understandings, decision-making, emotional and intellectual functioning, and behaviors. They formed a permanent association for the person, though they remain unconscious.

One can only conclude that the influence of past experiences on present-day TFA depends on the specific issues and must be individually determined.

# CHAPTER IV QUESTIONS

1.  What traits do you see in yourself?

2.  What do you particularly like about yourself?

3.  What do you not particularly like about yourself?

4.  Do changes in your physical state of well-being impact your TFA?

5.  How does your overall outlook affect your understanding of PSC?

6.  What repetitive thoughts are upsettings to you?

7.  What negative thoughts impact your ability to get things done?

8.  What painful feelings make it hard to function?

9.  Are your problem-solving approaches effective?

10. What steps do you take to resolve difficulties in your personal life?

11. What can you do to make work more satisfying?

12. What memories of the past replay in your mind and impact your TFA?

# V.

# EMOTIONS

Whether one directly experiences strong feelings or witnesses them in others, the impact can be overwhelming, as captured in the following excerpts from poetry, cinema, and literature:

> "Fierce as a dog with tongue lapping for action, cunning as a savage pitted against the wilderness.... Under the terrible burden of destiny laughing as a young man laughs, laughing even as an ignorant fighter laughs who has never lost a battle.... Laughing the stormy, husky, brawling laughter of youth...." (Carl Sandburg, from the poem, *Chicago*)

> "Remember, Red, hope is a good thing, maybe the best of things, and no good thing ever dies." Quote from Andy Dufresne in a letter to Red. (from the movie, *The Shawshank Redemption*)

> "You people with hearts, have something to guide you, and need never do wrong; but I have no heart, so I must be very careful." And then later: "I shall take the heart. For brains do not make one happy, and happiness is the best thing in the world." Quotes from the Tin Man. (from the book, *The Wizard of Oz*)

The external world of PSC and the internal processing of those events collide, creating feelings and responses in the process. Joy and bliss, warmth and love, rage and fury, panic and dread, melancholy and despair, frolicking and feeling high on life—all are examples of emotional connections (cathexes). Without them, a human being would be little more than a computer taking in and analyzing data. Every emotional response involves something central to the person. That something can motivate a person to do almost anything or demoralize one into doing absolutely nothing.

**Emotional Expression**

Emotional expression is distinct from thought and action in several ways. A person reveals one's emotions through reactions, traits, states, flow, and remembrances, each with the following features and implications:

- *Emotional reactions.* A sudden surge in feelings involving the element of surprise or a response to a series of events where the emotions have been building up. They are reflexive by nature, a reply to a perceived change in a person's life or perhaps a misperception or misinterpretation of events. For example, a person might overreact with anger because one feels disrespected by somebody who did not have that intention. The moment one responds with emotion to a PSC may have immediate significance with long-term implications or quickly come and go like a summer wind.

- *Emotional traits.* Enduring and ingrained feelings in one's character, unconnected to a particular PSC. A person who is usually peaceful and relaxed displays *emotional traits* that differ from those with an anxious disposition. Some individuals may appear cheerful most of the time, whereas others more commonly express anger or depression. *Emotional reactions* and *emotional traits* are linked together; when emotions are stable, a person is less reactive.

- *Emotional states.* Transient feelings, commonly brought on by a person's physical condition. Examples include excessive alcohol consumption, drug usage, and some acute medical illnesses, which can significantly affect mood depending on personality, situation, and circumstances.

- *Emotional flow.* Inwardly felt or outwardly demonstrated, a merging of one's feelings with the thinking process that may be sudden and spontaneous or reflective and deliberate. It is not a characterological condition or a product of a distressed physiological state. Whether long-lasting or a fleeting moment, *flow* may have significance or merely be musings of a person's casual observations. These feelings may be bittersweet, blissful, or overwhelming, involving relationships, grand opportunities, or journeys of the imagination. *Flow* may morph into a trait and become a firmly established response.

- *Emotional remembrances.* The continuing presence of feelings—tied to specific PSC—although there has been the passage of time in minutes, hours, days, or years. Perhaps one is engendered by a wondrous feeling, revisiting that spring day walking with a new love. But painful emotions, including grief and loss, disillusionment and failure, jealousy and resentment, may also enter in and endure. The events that inspire these emotional remembrances can have a pervasive effect beyond their initial impact.

## Emotions' Underlying Principles

The core precepts of emotional responses are as follows:

- *Emotional discharge/catharsis.* Some believe that merely expressing one's feelings will resolve troubling issues. While it is not helpful to hold emotions inside, it does not necessarily follow that expressing those feelings will sort them out and settle them. Sometimes, outward demonstrations only reinforce the distressing sensations and uncomfortable feelings. For example, continually grieving—seemingly without end—does not help a person work through a loss. Similarly, a person who vents anger may become even more incensed as that emotion builds on itself. A cathartic discharge—directly, loudly, and forcefully expressing one's feelings—will not alone resolve CTMI. A cognitive-emotional connection needs to occur.

- *Emotional combinations and shiftings.* Emotions are not separate, distinct, or disconnected. Although they are often defined and described one at a time, a typical emotional response is a blending of feelings. Rage, anger, jealousy, panic, fear, melancholy, worry, anxiety, depression, and the entire spectrum of emotions may combine, with even four or five feelings occurring simultaneously. These mergers of emotions, continually shifting with a different grouping of feelings arising within minutes, are the rule rather than the exception. Like a simmering stew in the kettle of one's personality, unique emotional experiences may be created and expressed.

- *Emotional depths.* The more potent the emotion, the stronger the cathexis. The intensity and fluidity of particular emotional *reactions, traits, states, flow,* and *remembrances* will depend on natural inclinations, CTMI, and the PSC, varying in the following ways:

  - *Explosive.* Random, crude, and impulsive.

  - *Undisciplined.* Reactive and spontaneous, including passionate responses.

  - *Proportioned and measured.* Steady, rhythmic, thoughtful, prudent, and appropriate.

  - *Limited.* A minimal response or no response at all.

- *Emotional individual differences.* Some people are naturally more emotional than others in their inner experiences or outer demonstrations (see *Emotional traits* on page 46). Biological predispositions, life experiences, and *spiritus* all have an impact. As a person passes through developmental periods and engages in significant life events, the effect of inherent tendencies becomes more apparent. For some people, relatively minor stimuli can set off emotional responses, while strong stimuli may elicit no reaction in others.

- *Emotional internal responses.* A strong emotional reaction can occur from simply thinking about an event. Anticipatory anxiety is one example of a person experiencing fear and dread over a future involvement with PSC.

- *Emotional chronicity.* People differ significantly in their emotional experiences and expression. A person's emotional responsivity reflects one's unique personality—expressed across a broad spectrum of life events—as exemplified in long-standing tendencies of anxiety, depression, or anger.

- *Emotional visceral quality/raw emotions.* The physical quality of emotions—a facial expression, handshake, or tone of voice—is revealing and often more potent than the words spoken. The particulars of these physical displays may be the result of the following:

  - *Behavioral patterns that have become ingrained.* A person engages in repeated actions over a long period of time with no premeditation or deliberate motivation to convey a particular message. These emotionally laden responses may merely be long-standing habits.

  - *The unconscious motivation that is operating.* A powerful emotional undercurrent may show itself in physical mannerisms that may or may not be consistent with a person's feelings on a conscious level.

  - *A person consciously attempts to deceive another but cannot suppress one's true feelings.* Unable to control all body language, one gives away the actual beliefs held.

- *Emotional consequences.* Overly emotional reactions can result in devastating outcomes, such as being fired, disowned, arrested, or sued.

- *Pseudo-emotions.* Virtual reality has become an integral part of daily life in the modern era, at least in wealthy, highly industrialized countries. Indulgence in pastimes that involve flights of imagination—with illusions and fantasies playing an outsized role in a person's daily life—has some of the characteristics of *emotional reactions, traits, states, flow,* and *remembrances.* Fantasies about people, situations, and circumstances (PSC) involve pseudo-emotions whereby a person may withdraw into an inner world and escape having to deal with everyday stressors and the consequences of one's actions. A person has a measure of control in virtual realms, finding "fulfillment" via vicarious thrills, make-believe achievements, and pretend relationships. But whatever emotions one experiences are particular to that domain and do not likely correlate to "real" life. Similar to recalling the emotions felt in a dream, one certainly feels something, perhaps even overwhelming anxiety, anger, or sadness, at least momentarily. But it is not the same emotion experienced in one's waking hours when feelings have depth and a visceral history attached to them. No one would argue the profound difference between *imagining* being in a war and *actually* being in one.

**Subtypes of Emotional Reactions**

Whether expressed or kept inside, emotions vary in the following ways:

- *Emotionalism.* Extreme emotional responses beyond what would generally be considered reasonable or appropriate. They are typically chronic conditions, not brief flare-ups, as exemplified in extreme reactions to environmental triggers, including rage, deep depression, severe panic, debilitating anxiety, and paralyzing fear. External events may play only a minor role in the person's response; unconscious conflicts, traumas, or malevolent identifications (CTMI) create the fertile ground where emotionalism takes root and becomes an automatic response regardless of PSC.

Emotionalism does not always show itself; it ebbs and flows, an ongoing in-and-out of emotional responses. It may take little provocation for a sudden, extreme reaction in which the person appears to have "lost one's mind." Having lost the ability to reason, at least temporarily, the person seemingly has little or no control over emotions.

- *Feigned emotions.* Acting. A feigned emotional response is a consciously thought-out performance to manipulate and fool someone. Although the person's behavior suggests genuine feelings, the brazen and fragrant attempts are to deceive and mislead. Possible motives include gaining sympathy, disrupting communication, or confusing and controlling PSC.

- *Hysteria.* Overreactions or over-dramatizations. Hysteria is the product of unresolved CTMI; behaviors may be volatile and extreme. Conduct and demeanor are highly manipulative, but not to the same degree or manner as feigned emotions. Hysterical responses are theatrical; they may also be seductive and provocative. Individuals with these responses present an exaggerated persona (the image a person displays to the outer world, which may be significantly different than the internal thoughts and feelings), often seeking to be the center of attention and recognized as special. They typically want others to like, admire and notice them, but their relationships tend to be superficial. They talk in vague generalities, lacking detailed knowledge of what they speak as they weave conflicting and inconsistent stories together.

- *Hypersensitivity.* Easily offended, with extreme emotional reactions, and becoming overwhelmed when exposed to the slightest hardships. The person has likely experienced insult, trauma, or humiliation somewhere along the way. Or, perhaps one was sheltered in the early years and not exposed to life's challenges.

- *Insecurity.* An inability to stand up for oneself that permeates the entire personality. Unsure of oneself, a person is easily intimidated and often shows little strength of conviction. Self-doubt, uncertainty, hesitation, anxiety, fear, and panic are all expressions of insecurity.

- *Negativity.* Continually finding fault with oneself, others, situations, or circumstances. Negativism is adversarial, pessimistic, cynical, and complaining. It creates a gloomy outlook that expands *pathos*'s influence, allowing emotionalism to become deeply rooted in TFA. Negativism results in alienation from others, with a vicious cycle ensuing, creating yet more negativity.

- *Rebellion.* Opposition to societal standards. Rebellion (antiauthoritarianism) represents an assault against conventionalism and the establishment; it tends to come from one of the following backgrounds:

  > *A home and a community that has indulged the person.* This environment has only "the best" schools, houses, cars, and vacations. An existential crisis may follow; the person rejects all that came before, adopting an opposite stance against the establishment.

  > *An upbringing that includes harsh punishments and family dysfunctions.* A person may become reactionary due to mistreatments, with significant anger and distrust becoming a deep part of one's character.

  > *A home environment that encourages antiauthoritarianism.* The parents have issues with authority figures and are outspoken in their views.

- *Inhibition.* The suppression of TFA involving self-imposed restraints, restrictions, and mental blocks, driven by fear of failure, consequences, humiliation, or the unknown. However, an inhibited person, on occasion, may do the opposite, acting boldly and aggressively in contrast to the fear and uncertainty felt.

• *Empathy.* Forming an emotional connection to another's experiences, sharing the other's joy and sorrow, pride and celebration, struggle and strife. It is not an intellectual exercise, as the linkage is visceral and emotional.

• *Passion.* A strong emotion that may help or hurt one's relationships and prospects for success. It entails high energy, enthusiasm, intense drive, devotion, and deep-rooted commitment and connection to a person, activity, or special interest. Passion may also involve "the fiery" emotions—rage, fits of anger, explosive outbursts. As extreme as they seem, these responses may prove useful when quick, decisive action is required. Not falling prey to the depths of emotionalism—with its chronic characterological features—is essential if a person is to avoid losing control of TFA. (see description of passion in Chapter VII, Sources of Energy)

## Emotional Responses to Traumatic Events and the Stresses of Everyday Life

Stress is a conglomerate of environmental conditions; it is a press consisting of difficult PSC combined with the internal workings of a person's mind. Painful and disruptive emotional encounters are a large part of the human condition. Some people have a high tolerance for the pressures and strains the outer world inflicts upon them, while others quickly succumb to these tensions. A person's experience of stress is continually changing, dependent on the particulars of the events taking place and one's personality. Traumatic events and the stresses of everyday life reveal the individualized nature of one's response to PSC and affect the personality in the following ways:

- *Traumatic experiences.* Whether physical or psychological, trauma's effects may be potent and can continue to cause psychological reactions, with post-traumatic stress disorder (PTSD) widely recognized as the most common example. PTSD may include flashbacks, in which a person reexperiences the highly stressful event, consisting of images, memories, and emotional reactions tied to these past traumas. When traumatic experiences are not resolved but blocked, censored, or edited, they eventually reappear when triggered by an image, thought, memory, or encounter. Suddenly, those experiences, typically laced with fear, overwhelming anxiety, and panic, are back in full force and can be debilitating and emotionally exhausting; physical symptoms may persist.

- *Everyday incidents.* All experiences have an emotional connection, whether it be trivial or profound. A type of conditioning occurs that results in the formation of associations. When a person is later exposed to certain PSC, even if only somewhat similar, a re-experiencing of the same emotions may occurs.

- *Emotional remembrances.* Flooding back into the personality, they may be more problematic under the following conditions:

  > *PI, II, CI, and TI are fragmented and inherently negative in outlook.*

  > *Pathos is strong and dominating, with emotionalism destabilizing the personality.*

  > *Directives are unbalanced, resulting in obsessions, compulsions, and addictions (OCA).*

# CHAPTER V QUESTIONS

1. What emotions do you commonly experience?

2. Do you express these emotions or keep them inside?

3. Do you emotionally overreact, and if so, what form does it take, and what tends to set it off?

4. Are you easily offended, and by what?

5. Do you have trouble standing up for yourself?

6. Do you tend to overreact to the conventional norms of society?

7. Do certain PSC emotionally inhibit you, causing your TFA to freeze up?

8. Are your relationships emotionally rewarding, or is something lacking?

9. Do you sometimes experience an emotional high and intense feeling toward a person or activity?

10. Have you had traumatic experiences that still affect you now?

11. Have you had other stressful experiences that impact you at this time?

12. Do memories rush back into your consciousness, and how have they influenced your TFA?

# VI.
## STATES OF AWARENESS

Morning has broken; one walks carefree through a forest, taking in its abundant beauty. Or perhaps one is mesmerized by a multilayered fountain in a bustling city's central park. On the dark side, a soldier feels intense anxiety when suddenly alerted to the sounds of enemy fire. These experiences reflect a high degree of consciousness; one is acutely aware of thoughts, feelings, and actions (TFA). But sometimes sensations or memories distract a person, compromise focus, diminish awareness, and impact what happens next.

### The Ebb and Flow of Conscious, Semiconscious, & Unconscious States

States of awareness or consciousness, interchangeable terms, describe the attempt to recognize and understand oneself and the world. Comprehending the realities of people, situations, and circumstances can only occur in gradations and approximations. These illuminations are transitory and fleeting, fluctuating according to internal experiences or external conditions. Conscious, semiconscious, and unconscious TFA can quickly shift and transform from one to another and back again; the features of each are as follows:

- *Conscious states.* Thoughts are deliberate, calculated, intentional, and purposeful. A person is fully aware of these images and ideas. Conscious thoughts are typically created through the use of words, either silently spoken or expressed aloud. Language, however, is not required for reflection; one can understand and solve problems through images and feelings.

    When conscious, a person is fully involved in an external sensory experience or an internal cognitive process. Examples of *external sensory experiences* include smelling freshly baked cakes in a bakery, hearing a dog bark, walking through a country field of wildflowers, and watching a baseball player round the bases after hitting a home run. Examples of *internal cognitive processes* include thinking about what to make for dinner, solving a complex math problem, and imagining one's favorite vacation place. External experiences and internal processing may involve problem-solving, focused attention, imagining, planning, and analyzing.

- *Semiconscious states.* One is not fully alert to internal thoughts and feelings or external actions and events. Perception, recognition, and understanding are only partly engaged; thought processes lack consistency and constancy. Semiconscious states are likely to occur under the following conditions:

  › *Fatigue.* Overwork or overstudy, sleeplessness, and chronic or acute physical illness can impact one's energy level.

  › *Alcohol or drug intoxication.* Attention span and cognitive functioning may be detrimentally affected by occasional or frequent usage of these substances.

  › *Pain.* Physical discomfort can reduce a person's capacity for sustained concentration.

  › *Neurological and neuropsychological brain disorders.* They can impair concentration and all cognitive processes. For example, dementia eventually causes significant intellectual dysfunction and extreme impairment in awareness.

  › *Learning dysfunctions.* Learning disabilities, attention deficit disorders (ADD), and attention deficit hyperactivity disorders (ADHD) can affect one's ability to concentrate, communicate, and relate to others.

  › *Daydreaming.* Fantasizing and imagining can affect a person's focus and ability to remain conscious. Although fantasy play can be a creative expression and an act of exploration, it may still serve as a distraction.

> *Ongoing personal problems.* Preoccupations affect a person's ability to concentrate on the tasks at hand. Examples can be found in everyday issues, including work difficulties, family and marital conflicts, academic troubles, and legal concerns.

> *Emotional reactions.* These reactions can be physically and psychologically draining, making it difficult to concentrate or solve problems. Examples include debilitating anxiety, anger, depression, and panic.

• *Unconscious states.* Ideas and images are uncertain and out of focus when one is unaware of TFA. A person's understanding of himself, people, situations, and circumstances may be blocked. Some unconscious states have an underlying motive, such as insulating the person from uncomfortable or painful emotions, while others do not. An unconscious transformation of CTMI may happen that can be either of a healing nature or a setback.

Not all unconscious actions result from blocking psychological discomfort or forbidden thoughts. With the continual repetition of TFA, unconscious associations may form because a person no longer pays attention to what one is doing. When minimal concentration or contemplation with the PSC is present, one's TFA may become reflexive automations with no hidden agendas or emotional significance. Reinforcements resulting from the person's actions are incidental to the behavior's unconscious aspect. When conditioning occurs, the associations themselves direct behavior, and a person's motivations play a minor role or no role in the response. Examples include activities requiring minimal problem-solving, such as exercising, playing games, cooking dinner, listening to music, cleaning the house, washing the car, feeding the dog, and countless other daily activities.

Unconscious states may involve the blocking of conflicts, traumas, and malevolent identifications (CTMI), assimilation and consolidation of emotional and intellectual processing, associations formed through life events, or actions that express innate human responsiveness. These four unconscious processes involve the following actions:

> ➤ *The blocking of conflicts, traumas, and malevolent identifications.*

>> ○ *Unconscious, Type 1: the blocking of cognitive-emotional connections.* One is unable to remember something unpleasant that has happened. In tandem with *pathos*, this lack of recall operates unconsciously throughout the entire personality and is especially dominant in *directives*. As *pathos* evolves, so does the blocking of cognitive-emotional connections; they align, complement, and connect. However, a person can rarely disconnect from these bad feelings entirely, as some conscious remnants of CTMI remain. A person may continue to experience emotional discomfort because muzzled and muted material is unresolved and CTMI are operating on conscious and unconscious levels. Self-deceit becomes a chronic problem, with blocking now automatic and habitual.

>> With the blockage of cognitive-emotional connections, TFA that create psychological pain may momentarily vanish. They still exist but are not in the conscious mind. A person who has experienced CTMI may avoid, deny, conceal, or distort TFA. Parental rejection and criticism during the childhood years are the most common factors involved in *Unconscious, Type 1*.

>> The blocking of CTMI from consciousness principally occurs when TFA are of emotional significance. A nearly automatic and instantaneous shutting down of the person's awareness of those TFA occurs. Al-

though the person may seem reasonable and rational, significant unconscious CTMI are still present. A symbolic-psychological-emotional undercurrent is operating.

➤ *The assimilation and consolidation of emotional and intellectual processing.*

    o  *Unconscious, Type 2: the integration of cognitive-emotional connections.* Similar to *Unconscious, Type 1,* this level of consciousness involves TFA outside of ordinary perceptions and understandings that register on another level of awareness. *Unconscious, Type 2* differs from *Unconscious, Type 1* in that *Type 2* is a process of internal healing, with the emotional turmoil of CTMI at least partially resolved on an unconscious level. *Type 2* does not involve blocking aversive experiences, and a person is unaware of what is happening. Opposing and contrasting elements of the *psyche* consolidate through integration and synthesis; a person's inner character and inherent emotional strengths are the catalysts for these changes. This unconscious process may resolve emotional issues as one busily goes about the day or through dreams as one sleeps. The person's *psyche* integrates cognitive-emotional connections, reconciling CTMI. An example is when a person has a series of dreams that resolve, reunite, and soothe those feeling states. *Unconscious, Type 2,* can be nearly automatic and instantaneous, and a symbolic-psychological-emotional undercurrent is present.

    o  *Unconscious, Type 3: adaptation and adjustment of cognitions.* Outside of conscious perceptions and learning opportunities, unconscious processes can increase cognitive performance. The mind can sometimes integrate one's knowledge and experiences without deliberate or focused thought processes. A person can occasionally absorb and incorporate information already stored, modifying and transforming one's understandings. The unconscious mind can frequently combine complex materials above and beyond consciousness alone. An example is a person who has a mental block while struggling with a work project. When meditating, dreaming, or just out of the blue in daily activities, one's thoughts consolidate, and the answer may appear. No symbolic-psychological-emotional component is present.

> ➤ *The associations formed through life events.*

>> o *Unconscious, Type 4: associations formed through the intentional or accidental pairing of TFA.* These unconscious actions involve associations created through classical conditioning. *Unconscious, Type 4, intentional type*, occurs when a stimulus (S-1) is deliberately paired with another stimulus (S-2), causing a person to respond to S-2 as if it were S-1. TV commercials exemplify *Unconscious, Type 4*, designed to form an association between the product with a desirable outcome. The typical example would pair the purchase of an expensive automobile with romance or success. Automatic and without thought, these associations are fueled by excitement, enthusiasm, and enthrallment. Prescription drug use that results in good health, a great social life, and joyous family gatherings is another pairing frequently observed in advertising.

>> In everyday life, there are countless examples of *Unconscious, Type 4, accidental type*. A person may work in a highly stressful environment (S-1) with another set of stimuli (S-2) incidentally associated with it, perhaps the organizational hierarchy, policy man-

ual, or even a specific architectural layout of the company. The person begins working for a new employer and may experience the same stress as the previous position. The association of S-1 and S-2 causes tension, even though the new job's environment should be more pleasant than the previous one. These kinds of associations can be firmly entrenched and highly resistant to change. Repeated TFA become automatic responses with no motivational significance attached to them. With classical conditioning, connections are formed simply by associations, with no symbolic-psychological-emotional undercurrent involved in the process.

o *Unconscious, Type 5: associations formed through intentional or accidental rewarding or punishing of TFA.* Instrumental (operant) conditioning increases or decreases the likelihood that a person will behave in a specified manner due to one's response. The person's TFA are reinforced via a reward or punishment based on the response (R-1) to a particular stimulus (S-1). When exposed to a different stimulus (S-2), no reinforcer to the person's response (R-1) occurs. Similarly, when exposed to that original stimulus (S-1) and the person responds differently (R-2), again, no reinforcer is forthcoming. Thinking may be minimal, with connections formed only through the reinforcements, responses at times becoming almost automatic.

An example of an *intentional reinforcer* is when a person who is not particularly hungry devours an entire bag of potato chips or a whole pizza. When first indulging, one is fully aware of these actions and choices. As time goes on, the pattern becomes an ingrained routine; almost in a trance, eating with little thought becomes a habit. *Accidental reinforcers* are both obvious and subtle. An example of an *obvious accidental reinforcement* is when a person receives additional pay for working overtime and takes on even more hours. An example of *subtle accidental reinforcement* is when a person receives praise for these efforts and becomes more conscientious. In both cases, the behaviors continue even when the person does not initially seek reinforcement. The associations determine the response, with no symbolic-psychological-emotional undercurrent playing a significant role.

o  *Unconscious, Type 6: connections formed through experiential learnings.* These connections are the product of TFA that are continually adjusted and adapted through life experiences. They may become automations, activities with no motivational significance attached to those unconscious TFA. Automations are behaviors that have become so ingrained that a person is unaware of one's actions that are now almost machine-like, effortlessly repeated, robotic.

   Experience, ability, intelligence, and effort can all operate unconsciously. An example is a person who has difficulty making friends because of a lack of interpersonal skills, resulting in complete unawareness of gaffes and social missteps. Another is a person who is lost in thought about work, school, or a personal relationship while driving, and suddenly realizes the need to turn at the up-and-coming intersection. Again, the consequences that result from the person's actions are unrelated to the unconscious aspects of the TFA. No symbolic-psychological-emotional undercurrent is present.

➤  *Innate human responsiveness.*

o *Unconscious, Type 7: the expression of instinctual urges.* All human beings have specific instincts, including sexual attractions, empathetic concerns, aggressive actions, and other biological urges. They may signify and express visceral gut reactions, seemingly without thought and not premeditated or planned. No symbolic-psychological-emotional undercurrent is present.

o *Unconscious, Type 8: dream states and the expression of imaginal connections.* Dreams are a form of thought and communication, whether or not the messages are received or understood. They are narratives that occur in words, images, and feelings. Dreams may involve *pathos* and *directives* blocking cognitive-emotional connections, masking the true nature of the dream's message and meaning. Other dreams flow through a person's *PI, II, CI,* or *TI*. Some are an expression of *spiritus* and may reveal one's inherent nature. Dreams are the most vivid example of the unconscious mind expressing itself. While a person is asleep, one tells a story with themes, emotions, dialogue, and drama; they may or may not have meaning attached to them. Dreams would seem strange and extraordinary if they were not universally experienced. How can the unconscious create the dream and then dream the dream?

Not all dreams are symbolically or psychologically meaningful. Some appear to be laden with significance, while others seem trivial. A dream may form from a long-ago trauma, while another from a minor argument the day before. Some are terrifying, while others express guilt, rage, love, or lust. Dreams may be recurring, often with themes of regret and loss. A person may also experience joy, sadness, or any of

a vast array of emotions but will not necessarily resolve CTMI. While there may be a release of tension,
dreaming can also increase it. Some dreams seem
to heal the *psyche* by connecting life events. A symbolic-psychological-emotional undercurrent may be
present, depending on the nature of the dream.

o   *Unconscious, Type 9: the natural expression of spiritus.*
Because a person generally goes about the routines
of daily life without paying attention to one's essential nature, *spiritus* primarily operates on an unconscious level. Focusing on those natural inclinations
can make *spiritus* less of a mystery and give a person
a fuller understanding of oneself. No symbolic-psychological-emotional undercurrent is present.

# CHAPTER VI QUESTIONS

1. Do you notice when you are not fully alert to your thoughts, feelings, or external events?

2. Do you sometimes go about your day almost in a trance, seemingly unaware of your TFA?

3. Do you tend to block out unpleasant memories?

4. Do conflicts sometimes seem to resolve themselves without any effort on your part?

5. Do complex issues and problems sometimes become understandable and resolve without working on them?

6. Do you frequently do something, almost on impulse, without giving it a thought?

7. Do you tend to form habits that become ingrained to the point that you are unaware of your actions?

8. Do you go with your instincts rather than premeditation or carefully thought-out planning in many of your actions?

9. Do you try to understand your dreams when you awake?

10. Are you sometimes unable to explain actions that are not in your best interest?

# VII.
# SOURCES OF ENERGY

Known as The Iron Horse, the steam locomotive in the 1850s allowed people to travel to faraway places in short amounts of time. Powering down the tracks at unprecedented speeds, it had seemingly harnessed the energies of the universe. Without this technological wonder, the village or hamlet in which one was born determined where one lived and died. The fuel running those trains liberated people from the limitations of small towns and settlements. Likewise, one could say that energy frees the human mind to explore one's inner thoughts and the vast possibilities of the world.

## Energy Levels and Personality

Emotions impact one's ability to maintain an energy level; they can drain the resources needed to navigate challenging PSC. Feelings beget still more reactions and become ingrained with a nearly automatic response pattern. Physical and mental exhaustion may occur. In contrast, one conserves energy when not overreacting to stressors but by dispassionately and deliberately resolving issues associated with them. Energy vacillates as emotions impact functioning in the following ways:

- *Emotional reactivity.* A person's tendency to overreact to minor inconveniences or disruptions consumes energy. But a predisposition to act quickly can be invigorating and lead to decisive action.

- *Physiology.* Some people are more "tightly wound" than others; they are prone to bodily-based stress reactions that include a variety of aches and pains. Muscle tension, in particular, is a common symptom that depletes energy. Meditation and various relaxation methods can calm the mind and rebalance energies by decreasing overreactions to PSC.

- *Psychosomatic reactions.* An unresolved emotional issue caused by internalized CTMI or external stressors can result in physical symptoms. A person may go from doctor to doctor seeking symptom relief to no avail. Addressing the underlying issues impacting the *psyche* can help a person work through CTMI, reduce physical symptoms, and free up energy.

- *Emotional propensity.* Partially determined by a predisposition, one experiences and expresses feelings about PSC, including trends toward anger, anxiety, and depression, to varying degrees.

- *Emotional experiences.* As exposure to stressful and painful PSC increases, one may develop a fixed emotional response such as anxiety, fear, panic, withdrawal, rage, or depression. The person continues to respond ineffectively to PSC, draining away energy. Sometimes, however, confrontations with difficult PSC can be a source of strength and resiliency, thus increasing one's overall energy resources for handling future problems.

- *Awareness.* When cognitive-emotional connections are blocked, a person may not realize energy resources are declining. As one begins to work through CTMI, blocking actions will likely dissipate, and energy levels will improve.

- *Balance.* A consistent value system conserves and develops one's energy resources. Unstable and contradictory *directives* do not provide a strong foundation for the personality's functioning.

**Energy Levels, Stress, and Pain**

Exposure to stressful PSC can deplete the body of its resources as it takes a toll on *PI, II, CI,* and *TI*. But taking on complex problems— even highly stressful ones—is also essential to one's development, without which the mind's capabilities cease to expand and may even decline. Herein lies the paradox: one needs both stress and a lack of it to preserve and replenish energy levels. An optimal degree of stimulation—varying from person to person—will enhance energy levels. A person may feel emotionally drained and completely worn out by an experience, while someone else finds an identical event stimulating.

**The Effects of Internal Noise on Energy Resources**

Internal noise is a form of mind cluttering; it occurs when a person continually gives negative messages to oneself. These may initially come from what one observed and experienced as a child, only later to be reinforced by the outer world. Internal noise affects a person's TFA on conscious and unconscious levels. With *conscious internal noise*, stressors tend to be intense and diverse. The person is aware of obsessive worrying, chronic anger, unresolved guilt, torturous regrets, deep sorrows, and unrelenting sadness. These thoughts can lead to mental exhaustion and physical discomfort, including headaches, stomach aches, chest pains, muscle tension, weakness, and fatigue.

*Unconscious internal noise* involves *pathos*'s influence and is akin to free-floating anxiety, malaise, or feeling on edge. It is disquieting and discomforting; a sense of unease creates diffuse tension that radiates throughout the body. An example of unconscious internal noise is waking up in the morning and feeling upset for no known reason. Unconscious CTMI, in particular, will reduce energy resources available for a person, allowing *pathos* to run wild. Unabated, *pathos* grows exponentially and dominates TFA. Emotionalism, a central quality of *pathos*, will continue to drain both physical and mental energies.

## The Effects of External Noise on Energy Resources

External noise is the stress from PSC that varies in its significance and impact on energy resources for each person (see Chapter III, The Environmental Press: People, Situations, & Circumstances). It comes from the following:

- *Vibrations.* The world has gone from the sounds of nature to the sounds of machines.

- *Technology.* The mechanization of work environments often leaves people feeling disconnected from their roles and alienated from their coworkers. For good or for bad, with or without awareness, technology impacts all aspects of daily life.

- *Political regimes.* The world's governments are complicated, confusing, and often destructive, causing stress for their citizens in the process.

## Developing Energy Resources Through Focus & Active Listening

The quieting of the mind allows a person to focus on listening. An "active inactivity" may then occur, with the recognition and acceptance that another's point of view also has merit. While there is a natural tendency to stand by one's positions, a person can reduce prejudgments and increase active listening by developing the following:

- *Introspection.* Self-reflecting can lead to understanding contradictions and confusions in the personality that may narrow one's views.

- *Recognition and understanding.* Strive to be conscious of the whole picture and recognize that PSC are complex and involved.

- *Patience and acceptance.* Show tolerance and acceptance. While worries, fears, and insecurities may not vanish, they will become less dominant in the thinking process.

- *Emptying of the mind.* Let go of obsessive thoughts and, in particular, their emotional links. Emptying is a release of CTMI built up over time that interrupts their continuing rampage on the human *psyche.* The person no longer holds onto painful mental processes that can intrude upon one's thoughts at any time.

- *Being present.* Direct thoughts on what is currently happening, minimizing internal and external noise.

## Expanding Energy Resources through Passion

Passion is an internal energy that can revitalize or deplete a person's energy resources. It is not inherently good or bad but depends on the specifics of one's reactions to people, situations, and circumstances (PSC). Its potentially explosive nature can be essential when overpowering an adversary. With the qualities of a double-edged sword, passion can cut both ways, resulting in the following favorable and unfavorable consequences:

- *Positive qualities.* Passion can drive a person or organization to grow and change, avoiding stagnation. When not bogged down with rules and regulations and left unbridled, it can propel development to new levels. Finding and implementing that change-of-course approach may be needed when the status quo doesn't work.

- *Negative qualities.* The powerful thrust of passion may interfere with considering critical issues and the consequences of one's actions. An overflow of vigor and blind fury can cause impulsive acts that are out of control, violent, and vengeful. At its worst, passion equates to brute force that is reckless, crude, and ferociously wild. Cults, lynch mobs, radicalized political movements, and all forms of extremism and fanaticism are examples of passion's energies gone mad.

# CHAPTER VII QUESTIONS

1. Do you tend to overreact to minor inconveniences or disruptions?

2. Do you feel "tightly-wound," with aches, pains, and muscle tension?

3. How do you react to internal conflicts and external stressors?

4. Have stressful and painful PSC drained off your energies?

5. Do your energies improve as you become aware of and work through conflicts, traumas, or painful identifications?

6. As your values become more consistent and thought through, do your energies improve?

7. Are you overly self-critical?

8. Do you sometimes feel on edge for no apparent reason?

9. Do you have a lot of stress in your life?

10. Do you reflect on contradictions in your personality?

11. Do you try to look at the whole picture of PSC?

12. Are you patient with others?

13. Can you let go of obsessive thoughts?

14. Do you attempt to direct your thoughts to what is currently happening?

15. How does passion express itself in your life?

# The Structure of Personality

# VIII.
# PERSONAL IDENTITY

As ten-year-old students arrive for their first science fair, excitement and anticipation fill the air. These budding scientists have put their hearts and souls into their projects in hopes of impressing the judges. In a different setting, youngsters jump for joy as they realize that the mysterious movement under the Christmas tree is a puppy; the bonding is instantaneously intense and changes them forever. Life events can powerfully impact and shape the ways in which a person sees and defines oneself. *Personal identity (PI)* includes characteristics that people do not share or have in common. It sets each person apart from another and makes one an original.

## Defining Personal Identity

*Personal identity (PI)* is the sense of who a person is and the ways in which one defines oneself. It includes the qualities and characteristics—the desirable and not-so-desirable—that distinguish one person from another in TFA. The person "stands alone," independent of a group, organization, or affiliation. *PI* includes a person's peculiarities, particulars, and distinctions: character, body image, persona, personal achievements, artistic expression, decision-making, and risk-taking. But *PI* is more than a list of accomplishments, occupations, military service, activities, hobbies, or schooling. It also includes the places one has been and the memories one has come to embrace, be they joyous, uplifting, bittersweet, or heartbreaking. Forming *PI* is a complex interplay between many sources and influences; the process is conscious and unconscious, euphoric and traumatic, deep in the past and as recent as this morning.

PI elicits a natural drive to protect the sense of who and what one is, with a fierceness and feral intensity to safeguard one's identity from continual concessions and compromise. This psychological armor allows a person to develop and embrace unique qualities that will enable one to demonstrate strength and resilience. The need to protect *PI*, however, can quickly become overprotection. A person may come to believe everyone is hypercritical and intruding on how one sees oneself. The person may become a "rebel without a cause" and continually react against societal norms. If transforming into *pathos*, *PI* can morph into unbridled ambition, insatiable competitiveness, self-absorption, uncontrolled aggression, and an asocial or antisocial style of relating.

**Subtypes & Variations of Personal Identity**

*PI* is a blending of the images one presents to the world and those deeply held inside. The varying aspects of *PI* include:

- *Style.* The manner and aura of a person's actions. Style especially distinguishes one person from another by its visual qualities. The clothes one wears, the car one drives, the hairstyle one sports, and the house one lives in, are all examples of style. It may convey an illusionary message, perhaps by design. Style may even involve a grand performance, as when a person uses a specific image to impress someone when attempting to make a sale.

    Style can be an expression of earlier life experiences that may or may not reflect elements of the personality. Some wealthy people drive jalopies and wear workers' clothes, while others of ordinary means operate luxury automobiles and dress in the latest fashions.

- *Body language.* Whether overtly communicated or covertly conveyed, physical movements are part of *PI* and reflect feelings; they affect how others receive a person's messages. Body language is always present and includes the following forms of communication:

> ➤ *Facial expressions.*

> ➤ *Hand gestures and arm movement.*

> ➤ *Pace and manner of walk.*

> ➤ *Posture.*

> ➤ *Tone, depth, and volume of voice.*

## Developing Personal Identity

A thousand and one experiences create *PI*; forging them together is a cumbersome process. Likened to forming a cobblestone path, a person's *PI* is the product of personal history—a colorful, bumpy, winding, and unique living of a life. The development of *PI* does not happen in a day, a week, or a year; it can even take an entire lifetime. One is usually not aware that *PI* is forming in a particular way.

How does *PI* come into being? In one's early days, the identification process is innocent, primitive, and unconscious. Beginning with instincts and impulses, with only the most rudimentary sensations and impressions, a person starts the process of defining oneself. These experiences provide that initial grounding and first glimmering of who a person is; they form the personality's foundation. Beyond this seedbed at its best, *PI* expands with the development of inner awareness, intellectual understandings, and reality testing, as follows:

- *Inner awareness.*

  > ➤ *Context.* To put one's history in perspective with reference points.

  > ➤ *Being still and present.* Having composure and alertness.

  > ➤ *Harmony.* Stability, consistency, and congruency in one's beliefs and actions.

> ➤ *Consciousness.* The degree to which awareness permeates the personality. One will be better able to integrate diverse aspects of identity when TFA are conscious.

> ➤ *Forthright and authentic.* Resolving the negativity and emotionalism of *pathos* and overcoming blocking, censoring, and editing.

> ➤ *Maturity.* Being responsible, dependable, adaptable, and flexible. A person considers all factors in attempting to understand people, situations, and circumstances (PSC). Maturity involves the suspension of hostilities, letting go of hypercritical attitudes, and limiting the fault-finding of oneself and others.

> ➤ *Moral reasoning.* Developing a conscience, the guiding principles to distinguish right from wrong. Although spiritual beliefs and religious affiliations can be strong influences, all of a person's experiences will affect one's capacity for moral reasoning.

- *Intellectual understandings.*

  > ➤ *Knowledge.* A sense of what has come before, from the dawn of creation to the present day. An appreciation and acceptance of societal norms and a striving to understand world affairs are present.

  > ➤ *Perception.* Penetrating insights, a clear vision, and an in-depth understanding of conscious and unconscious motivations. A person has a keen awareness of oneself and involvements with PSC.

  > ➤ *Synthesis.* Integrating knowledge with a deeper understanding of life events and personal experiences.

- *Reality testing.*

  > ➤ *Objectivity.* Seeing things as they are, a dispassionate and

unbiased view of PSC.

> *Grounding.* Not becoming overly theoretical or abstract. The person is unassuming, straightforward, concrete, and factual.

> *Pragmatism.* A practical and unsentimental approach to resolving issues and problems.

> *Experiential learning.* Comprehension, even with minimal instruction or preparation, due to involvement and participation in an activity. On-the-job training is an example.

## Issues in Personal Identity

The following additional factors can add nuance and intricacy to the formation of *PI*:

- *Diverse experiences.* Integrating events and experiences into a coherent *PI* is complex and challenging when involvements are conflicting, incompatible, or inconsistent.

- *Conscious, semiconscious, and unconscious.* A person's ideas about oneself may be confusing and unclear, flaunting a positive view while conflicts, traumas, and malevolent identifications (CTMI) run rampant in the underworld of TFA.

- *People, situations, and circumstances (PSC).* A person may look at oneself in different ways depending on the particular set of conditions. When stress is minimal and life is going along smoothly, one may believe that one can do no wrong. But when the environmental press is especially harsh and forbidding, negativity may overwhelm *PI*. Then again, if a person can persevere under trying conditions, *PI* may develop exponentially. In 1888, Friedrich Nietzsche famously wrote, "Out of life's school of war—What does not kill me makes me stronger."

- *Time.* As one ages, the degree to which *PI* changes will vary significantly from person to person. Some people continually adjust, adapt, and modify *PI*, while others stay the same throughout their lifetime. These changes may reflect personal growth but can also signify instability in one's *PI*.

- *Consonance. PI* may or may not be in harmony with the other elements of the personality; a lack of balance may result in a *PI* that is disjointed and confused.

# CHAPTER VIII QUESTIONS

1. How do you see yourself?

2. How do others see you?

3. How do you present yourself?

4. What do you notice about your body language when interacting with others?

5. What have been the strongest influences in your sense of who you are?

6. What inner qualities do you see in yourself?

7. What understandings have helped you in forming an identity?

8. How have intellectual insights affected your identity?

9. Are you sometimes too hard on yourself?

10. What kinds of experiences are an important part of your identity?

11. How has your identity been affected as you deal with difficult PSC?

12. How has your idea of yourself changed over time?

13. Is your sense of who you are consistent?

14. How have personal problems impacted your identity?

15. How have your values influenced your identity?

# IX.
# INTERPERSONAL IDENTITY

Guadalcanal, 1942. On a scouting patrol, a young marine falls into a deep cavern filled with water and no way out. Another marine spots him, crawls into the cave's chamber, and saves his comrade's life. The two become lifelong friends.

Chicago, 1964. A 16-year-old boy catches a cab downtown en route to a job interview. The cabbie, full of life's wisdom, describes himself as "a happy man" because he and his wife just put their fifth child through college. Although it was only a ten-minute ride, the exchange with the driver replays in the passenger's mind, giving him a perspective on contentment and satisfaction that he takes into adulthood.

Interpersonal connections of all kinds can have a lasting and profound effect on a person's identity. Both accidental and intentional experiences with others shape this dimension of the personality, creating *interpersonal identity (II)* in the process.

## Defining Interpersonal Identity

*Interpersonal identity (II)* is the way a person comes to see and ultimately defines oneself through contacts, associations, and relationships. The particulars of people, situations, and circumstances (PSC) in one's life experiences create remarkable and singular relationships that powerfully impact *II*'s formation. These interactions reverberate through the personality; specific characteristics of the exchanges are then consciously and unconsciously absorbed, affecting *II* in the process. Even buried thoughts and feelings toward others find a way in. The quantity and quality of a person's interactions determine the degree of consistency in *II*'s makeup. In one's early years, connections with people strongly impact *II*, especially in the following settings:

- *Family relationships.* Consciously and unconsciously, a child's one-on-one relationships with parents and siblings can result in adopting their characteristics and developing *II.* When one becomes too close—or not close enough—to them, dependency issues may result. Identifications may result in extreme imitation of their behaviors or the taking on of opposite characteristics.

- *The school years.* Identifications can result in a person taking on the same or opposite qualities and traits of teachers or fellow students.

**Subtypes & Variations of Interpersonal Identity**

Whether momentary chance meetings that are fleeting or continuing relationships that last a lifetime, interactions with others can profoundly affect one's sense of who one is. As a person matures, one will be drawn to certain people and repelled by others. Either way, these experiences may shape one's character and personal qualities. The following types of relationships influence interpersonal connections:

- *Immediate and extended family.*

- *Close and personal.*

- *Romantic.*

- *Collegial.*

- *Human-animal.*

- *Casual.*

- *Business and work.*

- *Adversarial.*

- *Teaching and mentoring.*

- *Psychotherapeutic.*

## Developing Interpersonal Identity

*Interpersonal identity (II)* is primarily developed through contact with others, whether those interactions be positive or negative, affirming or destructive. Relationships transform a person's *II* by assimilating similar or opposite characteristics. Sometimes the identification process is straightforward, simply copying the other's TFA. But it can also result from contradictory connections that are seemingly incongruent and inconsistent. Combining and synthesizing these characteristics may prove troublesome, with many contrary elements not fitting together into a person's *II*. These paradoxical associations happen because a person is drawn consciously or unconsciously to some quality the other has, like strength, intelligence, or courage. An identification can occur whether the other is viewed as a hero or a villain, admired or loathed, sought out or avoided.

Direct contact with a person is not required to influence the development of *II*. Merely witnessing an event can be enough to leave a significant impression. *II* may also occur through the characters one "encounters" while reading, watching a movie, or simply hearing about someone's social involvements. Interpersonal connections—whether created by face-to-face interactions or journeys of the mind—affect the way relationships impact *II* in the following ways:

- *Communications.* The "how" of the message conveyed (the manner and tone) and the "what" (the words spoken) determine the meaning and significance of the communication.

- *Chemistry.* The way in which people get along affects the development of *II*. When rapport and intuitive understanding are present in a relationship, positive and affirming connections create a good feeling. However, "bad vibrations" between and among people can also permeate through situations and circumstances. A person experiencing negative chemistry across a wide array of people, situations, and circumstances (PSC) usually reflects an *II* of highly critical and judgmental characteristics.

- *Emotional connections.* Cohesion and kinship enhance a feeling of closeness and coming together but may or may not be humane and can range from being the best or the worst in human thoughts, feelings, and actions (TFA). The feelings one experiences in relationships affect *II*'s development more than the thoughts one has about them. The more intense the emotion, the greater the influence is on the development of *II*.

- *Societal standards.* A person acknowledges and understands established ways of thinking. Recognizing society's mores—its customs and conventions—is an essential component in the development of *II*. It gives a person the grounding needed to define oneself and navigate through the complexities of people, stuations, and circumstances (PSC).

- *Perception.* An obvious subjectivity is involved when one chooses to incorporate another person's characteristics into the *II*. One person may experience an individual as compassionate and nurturing, while another may see that same person as dominant and demanding.

Compatibility between the person and PSC will significantly impact *II*'s creation and development. When the qualities and characteristics incorporated into the person are significantly varied, the probability of confusion and contradiction in the identification process will increase.


## Issues in Interpersonal Identity

The particulars of PSC have a significant impact on a person's identity. Interactions form a feedback loop, flowing back and forth, shaping and reshaping a person's identity and affecting the ways in which a person sees oneself in the process. Continual shifting occurs as a person thinks and rethinks social encounters and feels one's way to a particular *II*. Over the years, the effect of these interactions is nothing less than profound. The characteristics of one's *II* echo and reflect those multiple and varied interpersonal experiences. They interact with the other elements of the personality in the following ways:

- *II and the other forms of identity.* The personality elements that define one's identity may not connect but go separate ways. Or a person's *II* may harmonize with *PI, CI,* and *TI,* demonstrating similar themes and avoiding confusion and contradictions in the makeup of one's identity. More likely, *II* will agree with one or more of the other forms of identity and be inconsistent with the rest.

- *II and pathos.* These two personality elements can be similar or entirely different in a person. For example, when one's relationships and *pathos* involve emotionalism, that quality will consistently be present in a person's identity. However, if *II* primarily demonstrates appropriate and measured interpersonal traits, while *pathos* reveals significant reactivity in relationships, confusion and contradiction will occur in the identification process.

- *II and directives.* *II* can involve connections to people with distinct and even opposing value systems. When one's *directives* are in conflict with others' values, *II* may show significant contradictions in its makeup.

- *II and spiritus.* *II* does not affect *spiritus* since *spiritus* is an unchanging element of the personality. *Spiritus,* however, impacts *II*'s development by influencing the kinds of relationships a person seeks.

# CHAPTER IX QUESTIONS

1. How have your one-on-one relationships with family members affected how you see yourself?

2. How do you go about forming relationships?

3. What has been the impact of close relationships on your sense of who you are?

4. How did your relationships with teachers and classmates influence your identity?

5. How has your involvement with pets affected you?

6. Have work relationships played a role in how you see yourself?

7. How would you describe the way you communicate with others?

8. Do you tend to establish a good rapport with others?

9. Do your relationships have a strong emotional component, or do you tend to be more standoffish and cerebral in your interpersonal connections?

10. Do societal standards play an important role in your identity?

# X.
# COLLECTIVE IDENTITY

Mission to Mars. February 18, 2021: NASA successfully lands Perseverance to explore the Red Planet. The team who created and developed this technological wonder watches with anticipation and anxiety, hope and prayer. They experience the "seven minutes of terror," as the entry, descent, and landing (EDL) phase occurs more quickly than the radio signals can communicate its status. Glory! Because of their collective energies, Perseverance and its attached helicopter, Ingenuity, safely arrive at their new home. Team members develop a unique *collective identity* through the sharing of this bold and historic venture.

## Defining Collective Identity

*Collective identity (CI)* represents the qualities and characteristics that develop through one's connections with groups. The more potent the emotional component of these interactions, the greater the influence is on *CI*'s formation. It is the product of core beliefs shared with others in various group settings, from families to communities to countries. In-person involvement is not essential as merely reading, observing, or thinking about a group and what it represents can play a role in *CI*'s development.

It is natural to want to belong to a group. Affiliations can reduce anxiety and alleviate feelings of isolation and alienation; they may offer a sense of security. A group's appeal sometimes comes from its promise to provide purpose and fulfillment in one's life. *CI* can represent the best of humanity—a commitment to a team working on a scientific project, a dedication to a platoon in the heat of battle, a pledge to stay the course when an organization is facing challenging times, or working long hours in a hospital's emergency room. *CI* potentially allows one to move beyond self-preoccupation and commit to a noble and farseeing cause.

*CI*, however, does not always result in effective, positive actions. Simply embracing "group thought" can be destructive to both the person and the group. When accepting the entirety of a group's essence and innermost tenets without discernment, one may become involved with profoundly disturbed organizations linked to radicalized political crusades, cults, terrorism, and other extremist movements.

Although both *CI* and *II* result from emotional connections, each involves a distinctly different form of social interaction. *II* develops from close friendships, romantic interludes, chats with the neighbor, and countless other interpersonal contacts. In contrast, *CI* forms from an idea or ideal that holds the group together.

### Subtypes & Variations of Collective Identity

Attraction or repulsion to any particular group varies from person to person. Common factors involved in the development of *CI* include:

- *Family involvements.* Beyond one-on-one interactions, which is an expression of *interpersonal identity (II)*, families also have a collective impact on a person, reverberating and influencing all members in unique ways.

- *Ancestral background and heritage.* One's roots can play a critical role in a person's identity.

- *Country, city, community, and culture, past and present.* A person's involvement and identification with nation and neighborhood, as well as the clubs, societies, fellowships, social circles, and the crowds in which one travels, all may have their influence on *CI*. But when disparities between one's current lifestyle and early background are present, conflict and confusion in *CI's* development may occur.

- *Occupational choices and commitments.* A person's life work often becomes an integral part of *CI*. The varied dimensions of the work experience, including the labor itself, the time and energy involved, and its perceived purpose and significance, influence the creation and expansion of *CI*.

- *Religious beliefs and involvements.* For some, faith and spiritual beliefs become the guiding forces that direct their lives. However, a person's actions and lifestyle may contradict one's convictions, leading to turmoil in *CI*.

- *Military service.* The military experiences of shared ventures and operations can significantly impact *CI*'s development. Even decades after one's duty, the shared commitment to fellow service members and the military itself can keep these experiences an essential part of *CI*.

- *Activities, interests, and undertakings.* Pastimes and avocations including sports, hobbies, amusements, games, and volunteer commitments involve group interactions that can impact *CI*'s makeup.

## Developing Collective Identity

When group involvements with distinctive and enduring qualities are at odds, one may lose perspective of those connections. Conversely, one's identity will be more stable when the various associations are integrated and aligned, making identifications coherent and consistent. The following characteristics determine the degree to which a person's identifications will lead to a *CI* that is congruent and harmonious:

- *Ethos.* The central features and qualities of a group that stir one's attraction include:

> ➤ *Power and control.*

> ➤ *Artistic expression.*

> ➤ *Hostility and aggression.*

> ➤ *The natural world.*

> ➤ *Humanistic causes.*

- *Quantity.* Conflict, confusion, and contradiction within one's *CI* increases as the number of themes grows. Stability and consistency are compromised. Conversely, cohesion and clarity in *CI* are more likely present if an individual has fewer group identifications.

- *Intensity.* The emotional significance determines which themes will be foremost in *CI's* development.

- *Disposition.* A group's fundamental or underlying value becomes part of a person's *CI.* Although a degree of subjectivity is involved in casting a value judgment, destructive and constructive groups exist that warrant these characterizations:

  > ➤ *Destructive.* Examples include the Nazi Party, the Ku Klux Klan, Hell's Angels, terrorist organizations, criminal gangs, and totalitarian states. These groups typically engage in actions contrary to the positions they claim to hold.

  > ➤ *Constructive.* Examples include organizations that champion charitable, educational, scientific, or literary causes. Bureaucratic and political influences, however, may compromise what those groups purportedly stand for—causing confusion and contradiction in the identification process—and affect *CI's* development.

## Issues in Collective Identity

*CI*'s relationships with the other personality elements are complex and may often be contradictory and inconsistent. Furthermore, all other forms of identity, including *PI, II,* and *TI,* may be momentarily suspended when the alliance with a group becomes central and unshakable in a person's life. *CI*'s linkage to *PI, II,* and *TI* often occurs in the following ways:

- *CI's connection to PI and II. CI* can overwhelm *PI* and *II,* even to the point that they seem to barely exist. A strong *CI* may imply that *PI* and *II* are particularly weak, exemplifying their complicated and, at times, antagonistic relationship. These three forms of identity may work in concert and complement each other or clash in opposition. Any of these elements may dominate a person's sense of who one is and what one stands for at varying times, causing the development of the following types of relationships:

  - *Complementary. PI, II,* and *CI* have a commonality that creates harmony in one's identity. An example is when a person's *PI* and *II* display strength and purpose, while *CI* shows involvement with groups that demonstrate decisive action. Another example is when *PI* and *II* exemplify calm and dependability, as *CI* connects with consistent and reliable groups.

  - *Contradictory. PI, II,* and *CI* can also appear inconsistent and in conflict. A person's *PI* and *II* may be complacent and retiring, while *CI* gravitates to aggressive and dominant groups. Or, a person with a *PI* and *II* that are generous and warm may have a *CI* strongly attracted to controlling and authoritarian groups.

- *CI's connection to TI.* They may seem in line with each other and appear indistinguishable, especially in matters of faith and its practice. An example is a person who actively participates in a particular religion and, at the same time, has an abiding faith in God. But *TI* and *CI* may also be in opposition. An example is a person who participates in manipulative and destructive group activities while expressing a belief in an all-loving God and a desire to adhere to the sacred doctrines of one's faith.

- *CI's connection to pathos.* They may or may not reflect each other, as follows:

  ➤ *Direct linkage. Pathos* and *CI* may be consistent. An example is when *pathos* is hostile and rageful, and *CI* flows into aggressive and dictatorial groups that reinforce those traits. Another example has *pathos* displaying a dejected and defeated state, with *CI* drawn to groups that show aloofness or apathy.

  ➤ *Direct opposition. Pathos* and *CI* may also be in opposition. An example is *pathos* being passive and withdrawn, while *CI* connects to groups in a daring and defiant manner. Or *pathos* may be judgmental and hypercritical, while *CI* is compassionate and benevolent. The identification process demonstrates the reciprocal and coordinated relationship with *pathos.* In the first example, the person draws strength from the group's arrogance, while in the second example, involvement in the humanistic qualities of the group lessens *pathos's* hold.

- *CI's connection to directives.* While there are commonalities between *directives* and *CI,* they are not the same. *Directives* are a distilling of principles and motivations from the entire personality that come together to create a value system. *CI,* in contrast, includes idiosyncrasies, rituals, and activities particular to group involvements. Thus, *CI* takes on a group's qualities and characteristics, while *directives* consist of one's value system.

- *CI's connection to spiritus.* A person may attach to particular groups because of the continuous influence of *spiritus*. Its sway and impact may be unconscious, but becoming more aware of the nature of *spiritus* will enhance a person's ability to choose groups that complement personality and foster growth.

# CHAPTER X QUESTIONS

1. What group connections and commitments have you found fulfilling?

2. What do these group affiliations have in common?

3. How have they impacted how you see yourself?

4. Have you felt intensely aligned with these groups, or have the alliances been relatively mild and fleeting?

5. Have you broken off your ties with groups because they proved inconsistent with how you saw things?

6. How have your associations changed over the years?

7. What has been the impact of family involvements on your identity?

# XI.

# TRANSPERSONAL IDENTITY

Among religious beliefs held worldwide are the "Big Five": Christianity, Islam, Judaism, Hinduism, and Buddhism. Archaeological evidence suggests that humankind's connection to a deity goes back to ancient times. Prayer and ceremonial participation demonstrate reverence and commitment to sacred teachings. Strong identification of this kind has led some individuals to suffer persecution and death rather than renounce their beliefs.

## Defining Transpersonal Identity

*Transpersonal identity (TI)* is a person's identification with a non-material reality, typically involving an intrapsychic connection with God, the cosmos, or another spiritual domain, none of which can be directly known, primarily resting on faith and spiritual intuition. When the connection is strong, a person experiences a transformation in which one's spiritual essence becomes central. It may envelop the person and radically change the understanding of oneself and perceived place in the world.

*TI* is potentially an identity game-changer, as it can overwhelm, override, overcome, and outdo *PI, II,* and *CI. TI* can become *the* identification, rendering the other forms relatively insignificant and meaningless. Spiritual involvements may enhance a connection with all humanity or cause one to embrace radical and extreme doctrines of exclusion. *TI* may not be grounded in everyday realities, resulting in a vulnerability to bizarre and irrational beliefs.

But *TI* will not necessarily impact a person's TFA; it can play a minor role in one's life or remain entirely undeveloped. The other forms of identification may be more appealing, offering physical and tangible connections—here and now—on an earthly plane. The spiritual dimension may lack the grounding that a person finds essential.

## Subtypes & Variations of Transpersonal Identity

*TI* is not simply a reflection of a person's religious convictions or attendance of services; it is not a product of logical analysis or the rigorous study of books deemed holy. Doctrinal teachings may or may not be consistent with a person's spiritual connections. While exposure to different faiths and scripture readings may have a significant influence, *TI* often involves spiritual experiences and awakenings, taking one beyond the tenets of orthodox theology, traditions, and belief systems.

## Developing Transpersonal Identity

There is no specific formula for the development of *TI*; it can happen suddenly or evolve quietly over time. Its emergence can begin at any point in a person's life, with some experiencing a spiritual epiphany and evolution only in their later years. The development of *TI* includes the following factors:

- *Reality beyond the physical plane.* If a person believes that a spiritual realm does not exist, the very idea of *TI* will have no appeal and not develop. Some people would not even consider going beyond what is tangible until something of spiritual significance happens and causes them to reconsider earlier teachings and experiences.

- *Teachings in religious and spiritual subject matters.* Formal instruction in academic settings, attendance and participation at religious services, and independent study can reinforce *TI*'s development.

- *Prayer, meditation, focused attention, and imagery.* A person develops practices that open up new vistas, allowing transpersonal experiences.

- *Eureka experiences.* A person spontaneously becomes aware of spiritual realities and explores the experiences to a fuller degree.

- *Supernatural phenomena.* A person directly experiences a paranormal event that defies conventional explanations and seems to contradict the scientific understanding of nature's laws.

- *Everyday events.* In the development of *TI*, a person is drawn in by the following qualities of life experiences:

  - *Love and feelings of deep caring.*

  - *Protection, safety, and comfort.*

  - *Benevolence and acts of kindness.*

  - *Power, strength, control.*

  - *Aesthetic design and symmetry of the universe.*

  - *Truth and the meaning of life.*

**Issues in Transpersonal Identity**

*TI* interacts with the other elements of the personality in the following ways:

- *PI and TI.* PI is the product of sensory experiences including concrete events and involvements of everyday life, whereas *TI* results from intuition and impression entailing ethereal, celestial, and otherworldly experiences. *TI* is not a reflection of what a person sees and hears but what one feels and believes. When *TI* is strong, based on an unshakable, deep-seated faith, the person does not need objective data to support one's beliefs. While *PI* consists of one's entire history, *TI* often evolves through extraordinary moments involving euphoria, splendor, and transformation, causing a redefinition of oneself in fundamental ways.

- *II and TI.* Although *TI* is the product of spiritual connections and *II* of earth-bound relationships, they can still influence and reflect each other. When one seeks a personal relationship with God, one is more inclined toward involvement with others who share these views. Conversely, a person with a more intellectualized and abstract understanding of God is less likely to need these connections.

- *CI and TI.* Both may involve a search for meaning or significance, although neither necessarily embraces concern for humanity. With *TI*, the goal is spiritual fulfillment, whereas *CI* strives for enrichment through group involvement. *CI* may include the social elements of organized religion, participating in its ceremonies and rituals. A person will be naturally inclined to align with groups consistent with one's beliefs, further developing *TI*.

- *Pathos and TI.* A person may not be aware of inconsistencies between *pathos* and *TI*. When *pathos* is dominant, with inherent conflicts, traumas, and malevolent identifications, a person's *TI* may be contradictory and confused.

- *Directives and TI.* If a person's value system is unbalanced, motives can become extreme, leading to obsessions, compulsions, and addictions (OCA) that affect *TI* in the process. *Directives* become one-dimensional; a person's preoccupation and overfocus on a particular value may diminish the interest in experiences needed for *TI*'s expansion and maturation. But *TI* can also provide inner strength, helping a person overcome those preoccupations, leading to a more balanced value system.

- *Spiritus and TI.* While both involve a connection to a non-material reality, *spiritus* is already present from the beginning of one's life. It is primordial and pervasive, with an ongoing influence on the whole person. In contrast, *TI* is one path a person takes that may or may not affect the other personality elements. As *TI* develops, however, a better understanding of the nature of one's *spiritus* may occur.

# CHAPTER XI QUESTIONS

1. Do you believe in God?

2. How would you describe your spiritual beliefs?

3. How does prayer fit into your life?

4. How does your faith affect your feelings about yourself, others, and the world?

5. How did your spirituality first develop?

6. How has it changed over time, and does it continue to change?

7. Are your spiritual beliefs primarily based on intellectual understandings or an emotional connection?

8. Is your faith reflected in your everyday life?

9. Does your spirituality affect your relationships?

10. How does it influence your views of people and society?

11. Do your beliefs affect your values?

# XII.
# PATHOS

A popular theme in the science fiction genre is the premise that robots will become autonomous and rule the human race. But regardless of the remarkable technological advances of artificial intelligence (AI), automated machines will always be a synthetic and incomplete representation of the mind because they do not have the qualities of *identities, pathos, directives,* or *spiritus. Pathos,* in particular, with its composite of negative emotional states, has no allegiance to the logical thought processes displayed in robots. Crucial to fully understanding personality, *pathos* cycles through all aspects of being, altering one's perceptions of people, situations, and circumstances (PSC), impacting thoughts, feelings, and actions (TFA). It is the mind's wild card, an unpredictable component of personality ungoverned by reason.

## Defining Pathos

*Pathos* is an aggregate of emotionally charged aspects of the personality that causes an expansion of adverse, disturbing, and disruptive images toward oneself and others. It is a complex, a cluster of fixed ideas or attitudes that typically—but not always—originates in childhood, becoming habitual and maladaptive. *Pathos* is predominantly an outgrowth of *personal identity (PI),* gradually pulling away as it becomes an independent function of the personality. Fully grasping its nature requires understanding *pathos's* relationship with *PI*. As previously discussed, *PI*, primarily operating on a  conscious level, consists of beliefs a person has about oneself and the ways of fitting into the world. Accepting the ebb and flow of life, *PI* recognizes reality; it adjusts, adapts, and remains intact despite the trials and tribulations.

But then "along comes a spider"—*pathos*—the part of inner experience that is distressed and doubting, harmful and hostile. *Pathos*, functioning unconsciously, is like the *PI*'s evil twin, mirroring the unpleasant side of *PI*'s qualities and characteristics. *Pathos*'s reactions include raw feelings of inferiority and self-doubt, uncontrolled guilt and regrets, raging anger and panic, and deep depression. It is that part of *PI* that is vulnerable, fragile, conflicted, and emotionally unstable. Because of *pathos*'s unconscious nature, a person has less control of TFA when it dominates; reality testing is impaired, and the value system becomes unbalanced. In extreme cases, *pathos* can replace *PI* altogether. Common characteristics of *pathos* include the following:

- *Hostility.* Aggression is experienced and may be displayed in the following ways:

  > *Physically.* Open displays of anger and, in extreme cases, acts of violence.

  > *Verbally.* Confrontational abusive talk, including insults, name-calling, cursing, and put-downs.

  > *Passively.* Cooperative with and accepting of others on a superficial level, but with the tone of voice and body language revealing hostile intentions to demean and put down the other person.

  > *Internally.* Being unaware or only partially aware of the depth of hostility one feels toward oneself, others, or an institution.

- *Pessimism.* One views life through a "lens of negativity" with a cynical and distrustful outlook.

- *Empathic unresponsiveness.* Intolerance for others is evident with a minimal attempt at understanding PSC.

## Subtypes, Variations, & Developing Pathos

The extent to which *pathos* develops varies; it may expand to envelop the entire personality, or the strengths of one's personality may diminish or even prevent its growth.

Forged in large measure by negative experiences in childhood and beyond, *pathos* reveals itself through the "three-headed monster"—conflicts, traumas, and malevolent identifications (CTMI)—with emotionalism fueling it with definition, intensity, and vigor. The influence of *pathos* expands when its building blocks—CTMI and emotionalism—combine and interact. Each element alone can detrimentally impact one's life, but the compounding effects are even more overpowering. The following characteristics of *pathos* will disrupt, impede, and upset the personality structure and cognitive processes in profound ways:

- *Conflicts.* Disagreements within oneself or with others create a struggle over issues involving aggression, assertiveness, intimacy, achievement, ambition, trust, or independence. Internal disputes often begin with parent-child interactions, while others come into play later through a wide range of relationships. When blocked from consciousness, these contradictions are left unresolved. They recede into the background only to re-emerge later, triggered by PSC.

- *Traumas.* Distressing and disturbing experiences come in many forms, from physical assault to the less obvious affronts of everyday life that can also be overwhelming and devastating. The effects vary widely, depending on a person's sensitivities, toughness of spirit, and history of PSC. The experience of trauma happens on both conscious and unconscious levels. Consciously a person may feel upset at the time but only later experience a stronger reaction. Dreams, flashbacks, physical symptoms, and even serious illnesses reflect the effects of trauma on an unconscious level. Traumas, however, can also enhance a person's development of the following qualities:

> *Wisdom.* A person ponders frustrations and failures, gaining an understanding of weaknesses and vulnerabilities. One may also develop a deeper understanding of PSC that enhances the ability to face adversaries in the future.

> *Empathy.* With an understanding and appreciation of life challenges, one develops emotional perception, forgiveness, and compassion.

> *Inner strength.* Learning to persevere under challenging conditions, the person develops a deep resolve to fight on when all seems lost.

• *Malevolent identifications.* Powerful and intense connections to a person, institution, or idea lead to unprincipled, inhumane, or maladaptive TFA. Malevolent identifications differ from more typical identifications because they are intrinsically harmful, with toxic properties and jagged edges—course and crude aspects of the personality.

Malevolent identifications are connections "gone wild"; they are highly emotional and may completely overwhelm the intellect. Why would they take root if so fundamentally negative and disturbing? First, most malevolent identifications occur on an unconscious level. Second, these identifications result from experiencing something that pulls on a purely emotional level. Third, since the process does not follow a logical course, intricate and perplexing aspects can draw the person in, perhaps the very opposite of what one might expect. An attraction to particular qualities and characteristics—even if they are bizarre and overwhelmingly destructive—leads to the creation of malevolent identifications. The most common of these include the following:

> *Power, domination, and control.* Although rarely admitting it, people may have a fascination or admiration for

these qualities, as exemplified by their identification with ruthless authority figures.

> *Charm and allure.* While people might say they are not in awe of celebrities, they may be attracted to the Hollywood look of things and become star-struck, admiring and identifying with the "rich and famous" lifestyles.

> *Thrill.* A desire to be part of an exciting adventure involves going against the status quo, drawn to something ominous and dark.

> *Belonging.* Attraction to a group involved in violent activities may offer social status, stimulation, and a sense of inclusion and affinity. An example is when someone joins a gang or terrorist organization, fulfilling a need to be accepted and attached to something larger than oneself.

> *Grieving.* Excessive rumination about a bygone era or a person no longer in one's life can go beyond normal grief. The person continues to hold on to that loss, which becomes idealized.

> *Bureaucratic zeal.* Being caught up with one's rhetoric and ideas can take on a life of its own. For example, a person running an organization, or even a country, can become entrapped in one's own embellishments, obsessed with unnecessary and cumbersome details.

- *Emotionalism.* Even when not overtly expressed, extreme emotional reactions can become so entrenched that they dominate a person's life. One example is a child developing the parents' inner feeling states, as well as mimicking their tone of voice, facial expressions, body language, and speech patterns. Emotionalism flows through CTMI, making pathological conditions more pronounced and disruptive. While emotionalism is not the source of those disturbances, it is the energizing force propelling them. As emotionalism becomes even more extreme and out of control, CTMI may express themselves in more exaggerated ways, as follows:

> *Self-obsessed.* The person is overly concerned with possessions, money, job, and appearance; the entire focus is "what's in it for me." Self-preoccupation develops in the following ways:

> o *The prima donna complex.* The person is overindulged during childhood and treated as if one could do no wrong. *PI* develops poorly without sufficient boundaries or limits, and the person can become overwhelmed by idiosyncratic interests and preoccupations. With a lack of consideration for others' needs and rights, *pathos* can expand wildly.

> o *Extraordinary compensation.* One's identity rests entirely on personal achievements; doubts and uncertainty lead to overcompensation. Examples include believing one is the only person who could win the state science fair or score the winning touchdown in the championship game. But unlike the person with the prima-donna complex, the capacity for empathy may still be present.

> *Suspicious and untrusting.* Reluctant to take PSC at face value, one looks for hidden meanings and motives in the behaviors of others.

> *Inconsistencies.* Thoughts, feelings, and actions (TFA) conflict in irreconcilable ways.

> *Carelessness.* An overall lack of seriousness results in a neglectful, unstudied, and inattentive approach to relationships and activities.

> *Instability.* One displays a lack of self-control, impulsiveness, and reactiveness, possibly with fits of anger.

➤ *Inappropriate interactions.* An overly sensitive attitude becomes evident when a person reacts strongly to criticism, disapproval, or rejection.

➤ *Dependency.* The person demonstrates a passive role in relationships, over-relying on others to make decisions. When independent action is required, a fear response occurs. Submitting to others in exchange for their help or emotional support may temporarily reduce anxieties. During childhood and continuing into adulthood, these dependency issues can develop in the following ways:

   o *Co-dependency.* The parents may directly encourage a dependent relationship that then generalizes across PSC.

   o *Identification with a parent.* A child identifies with parents who are passive and dependent, and develops these same traits.

   o *Identification with an institution.* A dependent relationship forms with an organization; one expects special treatment in exchange for cooperation.

➤ *Perfectionism.* Striving for excellence has positive aspects, but perfectionism can result in multiple problems due to obsessive-compulsive ritualistic TFA. Stomach aches, headaches, fatigue and exhaustion, panic attacks, worries, and anticipatory anxiety may follow. Contributing factors in the development of perfectionism include parental expectations, with a child feeling pressure to achieve. A child may also react to parents that are passive and retiring, adopting ambitions that are driven and perfectionistic.

➤ *Domination.* An overwhelming need to control others commonly occurs from the following influences:

   o *Identification.* Taking on the characteristics of those

who are attempting to dominate.

o *Direct teaching.* Through a learning process, coming to believe that dominance is a desirable quality.

o *The modeling effect.* Observing these qualities in others and seeing dominance as desirable.

> *Antiauthoritarianism.* A person who identifies with oppositional behavior wants to challenge the establishment simply because it is there; one becomes a "rebel without a cause." A person need not be in a street gang or a terrorist network to be a rebel, but only have a disregard for society's norms. Organizations substituting for the family structure reinforce a rebellious attitude and a corresponding belief system. Antiauthoritarianism may form in the following ways:

o *Reaction and rebellion.* Overtly or covertly, the parents have formed an authoritarian family structure. A child may initially comply with parental demands but later rebel when new influences come into play. As an adult, one may then reject the parents' belief system and the norms of society.

o *Direct teaching.* The parents may encourage particular attitudes with statements including: "the government is bad" and "companies are always taking advantage of the workers."

> *Exploitation.* People equate to commodities with no intrinsic worth. The person has not matured and established a sense of right and wrong. One's interests are at the forefront; the exploitation of others develops from the following conditions:

o *Deep insecurities.* When lacking self-confidence and doubting abilities, one may follow others' dictates regardless of the moral implications of their actions or lack thereof.

    o  *Victimization by parents.* Lacking empathy and morals, parents take advantage of the child who then takes on exploitative traits.

    o  *Victimization by institutions.* The community and societal institutions convince the person that the world is a harsh and bitter place; negative and maladaptive attitudes and beliefs develop along with a cynical and hostile view of others.

➤  *Apprehension.* Fear, anxiety, and panic occur across the spectrum of people, situations, and circumstances (PSC). As a result, one may overreact and quickly forms associations. The following characteristics differentiate these three reactions:

    o  *Fear.* Reacting with dread and fright to someone or something, the person's response is individualized, concrete, and distinct.

    o  *Anxiety.* Apprehension is diffuse and scattered. With a build-up of tension, stressors mount and compound, causing emotional exhaustion.

    o  *Panic.* This state of alarm and trepidation frequently manifests itself physically. Someone or something startles the person who becomes overwhelmed and momentarily loses control of thoughts.

➤  *Skepticism.* Doubt, questioning, and disbelief characterize the personality. Nothing is taken at face value; the skeptic endlessly asks questions and is dissatisfied regardless of the thoroughness of the answers. The person may also be pessimistic, distrustful, and suspicious, imprisoned by obsessive-compulsive (OC) tendencies resulting in endless procedures, rules, and regulations. Characteristics of skepticism include:

o *Rigidity.* An unwillingness to be open and flexible in both thought and action with a reluctance to take a chance.

o *Poor judgment.* A lack of common sense in understanding, drawing conclusions, and making decisions.

o *Impracticality.* An overly theoretical approach to PSC, with an unrealistic and unfeasible problem-solving strategy.

o *Controlling.* A restrictive and rigid approach to interpersonal relationships, characterized by overdirecting and overmanaging others.

o *Procrastination.* An inability to get things done decisively, quickly, and without hesitation.

o *Poor interpersonal skills.* A lack of expertise in negotiation and compromise affecting the development of trusting relationships.

o *Poor decision-making.* An inability to troubleshoot or grasp the different parts of a problem.

**Issues in Pathos**

The insults, hurt feelings, dishonors, and disparagements of daily life may combine with CTMI and emotionalism to impact *pathos's* development. Because *pathos's* nature gives feelings precedence over thought, emotionalism becomes its central feature and flows through all of one's experiences with PSC. When the thoughts, feelings, and actions that follow are adverse, disruptive, and out of control, awareness of one's motivations is especially crucial. Understanding *pathos* in oneself and others can result in the development of penetrating insights into human motivation, be it obvious or subtle. Intellectual insights, however, do not guarantee the taming of *pathos*. Any aspect of *pathos* operating on an unconscious level cannot be quickly resolved or modified. It is self-perpetuating and highly resistant to change because of its raw emotional quality and the undercurrent of unresolved unconscious issues. Additionally, the continual interactions of CTMI with the other elements of the personality, along with everyday experiences, can reinforce *pathos*'s hold.

# CHAPTER XII QUESTIONS

1. What adverse emotions do you have toward yourself and others?

2. How do these feelings impact your life?

3. How do they affect the way you think about things?

4. Are your thoughts, feelings, and actions out of sync with one another?

5. Do you sometimes feel you are losing control of your emotions?

6. What inner conflicts do you notice, and are you working on them?

7. What distressing experiences have you had, and how do they impact you and your relationships?

8. Have you been drawn to someone or something that has negatively affected your life?

9. Do you overreact to minor irritants or displeasures with emotional outbursts?

10. In what ways do these overreactions get you in trouble?

11. Do you have difficulty trusting others, wondering what they're up to?

12. Are you too dependent on others when making a decision?

13. What extreme emotional responses impact your relationships with family, friends, and coworkers?

14. Are you too quick to go against the grain, overreacting and rebelling rather than working things out?

# XIII.
# DIRECTIVES

In Frank Capra's classic Christmas story, *It's a Wonderful Life*, George Bailey experiences moments of crisis that require him to define his values and act on them. He wishes to travel the world but ends up running a community bank. Because he refused a bribe that would have secured his future, he was able to help townspeople keep their homes. He considers ending his highly stressful life but instead decides to save another's. Throughout the narrative, George Bailey's actions reveal a man struggling to define and act on his values, demonstrating the crucial role of *directives* in life's drama. A person's willingness to sacrifice when passionately committed to a cause reflects *directives*, but a collection of cravings that come and go does as well. The values one embraces may seem insignificant and frivolous, or they can produce crucial and far-reaching actions that may even change the course of history.

## Defining Directives

*Directives* are guiding principles that each person adopts and lives by, not a simple checklist of values uniformly developed and applied. A person's goals, motivations, needs, and desires coalesce to form a value system; they are internal, intrinsic, and perhaps ingrained. Simply stated, *directives* are what a person values—the good and the bad—that direct one's life. The entire personality affects a person's values, and all elements of personality are affected by them.

While values can form from random events, they predominantly come through identifications which may be simple and straightforward or complicated and deep-rooted. They flow from a person's history: joy and sorrow, love and hate, elation and heartbreak, victory and defeat. Family and faith, people and places, culture and community, institutions of learning and wisdom of the streets, all affect how values form. Their characteristics include:

- *Conscious vs. unconscious values. Directives* are one's inner-most wants, operating on conscious and unconscious levels of TFA. Conscious motives allow a person to direct and change values. Conversely, a person lacks control of TFA when mo-tivations are unconscious, frequently caused by the blocking of cognitive-emotional connections. Unconscious values may be insidious and perhaps Machiavellian because of unresolved conflicts, traumas, and malevolent identifications (CTMI), or they may be of little consequence.

- *Reality and reality testing.*

  - › *Gnothi seauton (know thyself).* These words are carved into stone at the entrance of the Temple of Apollo at Delphi in Greece and are easier said than done. Does a person truly know oneself? Knowing requires not only understand-ing *PI* but overcoming the barriers that can impede full awareness of one's mind, including:

    - o *An unconscious life.* Blocking an array of negative emotional states can become an automatic process integral to how a person sees oneself. One may be-come entranced by self-appointed attributes, even though actions do not reflect them. An example is a bully using the glowing self-description of being a natural leader.

    - o *Inaccurate and distorted perceptions.* The person no longer sees things as they are. With minimal aware-ness, one misrepresents, exaggerates, or habitually lies. The person is unwilling to explore less desirable values and whence they came. Self-awareness is hard to achieve because CTMI continually filter through a person's self-image. Intellectual and emotional dysfunctions also affect perceptions. A person not in touch with TFA will show diminished judgment and impaired ability to analyze and understand.

> ➤ *To thine own self be true.* Authenticity, being true to one-self, is an awareness of who one is and what one stands for, and the courage to take appropriate action. Acting on one's values can leave a lasting impression and a powerful impact on others. It requires one to manage aspects of life that include:
>
>> o *Developmental stages.* Navigating specific periods in the life cycle.
>>
>> o *Crises or traumas.* Reevaluating one's life after a pain-ful experience.
>>
>> o *Awareness.* Understanding the elements of the entire personality.
>>
>> o *Experiences and events.* Engaging in life-changing activities.
>>
>> o *Identifications.* Experiencing connections that alter the personality.

- *Value clarification.* A person's quest to understand one's value system starts with detailing wants and needs. One may have to give up an idealized version of values when they do not reflect those central motivations accurately. Value clarification means coming to terms with inconsistencies in one's life and lifestyle, including:

  > ➤ *Proportionality.* A sense of harmony in *directives*.
  >
  >> o *The extent to which values reinforce each other.* Values may complement or contradict one another and dis-tort their original mosaic of qualities.
  >>
  >> o *When one or two values dominate.* Some values may

diminish in importance or never develop in the first place.

o   *Learnings from life experiences.* Adjustments allow a person to keep perspective and avoid obsessions, compulsions, or addictions.

➤   *Consistency.* Stated beliefs and actual behaviors in harmony, with congruency in thoughts, words, and deeds.

o   *Innermost Intent.* The outer image that a person creates for the world (the persona) is consistent with the thoughts, feelings, and the principles that guide actions.

o   *Willingness to act.* One's value system may require risking reputation, career, and lifestyle for a principle, a core value.

➤   *Clarity.* Being understandable and well formulated.

o   *Spelled out.* Values can be concrete or abstract. If they are excessively detailed, the meaning and significance of the values must be coherent and unambiguous. But, if they are overly theoretical, one must explain the values' practical implications.

o   *Weighting and ranking.* A person's ratings of wants and needs reflect their importance and significance. Some values may score a "10," others a "1," and still others a "5" or "6." Simultaneously, a few values may be at the top of a person's list, while others not ranked at all.

o   *The environmental press. Directives* may fluctuate; they may be fluid, flexible, and continually changing with PSC, or strongly adhered to regardless of the conditions.

o *Point of view.* Establishing a universal criteria for a value is somewhat subjective. Common sense and moral reasoning, however, do suggest that values need to be consistent, coherent, and well-grounded. For example, common sense indicates that a person should not engage in destructive behaviors involving oneself or others. Moral reasoning holds that integrity, fair play, justice, trustworthiness, honesty, and honor are all intrinsically good. Changes in a person's point of view can affect values as follows:

   ✓ *Perspective.* Looking at PSC from a particular viewpoint can result in adjustments in TFA and a reframing of the issues.

   ✓ *Radical renewal.* Adopting new values may require a complete reorganization of beliefs.

o *Integration.* Values need to be consistent with each other and with the personality as a whole. Without this blending of qualities, confusion and contradictions abound.

o *Mosaic of qualities.* Directives have many characteristics that form a distinctive pattern of one's needs and wants. Each quality has opposing features, and PSC can trigger a counterreaction in which a person may go from one set of needs and wants to another, often in direct opposition. If one has not experienced the necessary gradations in developing a system of values, *directives* can be like an on-off switch. With no "in-betweens," a person's values can become extreme and ingrained, especially when developed earlier in life.

o *The external world.* A person's interactions as one encounters various PSC reflect in TFA and impact values.

o *Awareness.* When *directives* are primarily unconscious, a person will have significant difficulty knowing one's values. Becoming a keen observer of TFA, allows one to uncover them in the following ways:

✓ *Understanding one's dreams.* Dreams will often reveal unresolved issues a person may have with values. While sleeping, the unconscious mind may create metaphors and images that can be made conscious and offer meaning and direction.

✓ *Recognizing the ebb and flow of consciousness.* Awareness of PSC continually changes, flowing through conscious, semiconscious, and unconscious states.

o *Development.* To understand the origins and development of specific values, a person must examine the connections among *directives*, CTMI, and specific PSC.

## Subtypes of Directives

A person will have many values, several of which overlap. Reconciling contradictory values that occur from conscious and unconscious influences is challenging. Although any want or need can become a value, the most common are as follows:

- *Earthly delights and discomforts.*

  ➤ *Pleasure and pain.* Generally speaking, a person seeks pleasure and avoids pain. A deeper exploration of these desires follows:

    o *Pleasure.* Feelings of enjoyment, fulfillment, ecstasy, bliss, merriment, comforts, moments of elation, delight, jubilance, celebration, and fun are examples. These experiences may result from interactions with others or through solitary undertakings. Pleasure is the zest of life—the entwinement in the world of sensations, movements, exhilaration, energy, and buoyancy. It is to have vigor and to be physically present. However, sampling the *Garden of Earthly Delights'* varieties will not always prove to be delightful. Pleasure can be overdone, grossly inappropriate, and outrageously indulgent. Hedonism and pleasure at the expense of others can cause obsessions and compulsions of every sort to run rampant. By relentlessly seeking gratification without reasonable limits, a person may become a mindless pleasure addict.

o *Pain.* Unpleasant experiences are an unavoidable part of life. Physical and psychological distress can range from mild discomfort, stress, or unease, to misery, heartache, and the depths of despair. Just as a person may continually seek pleasure in all its forms, one can also attempt to avoid pain at all costs.

With all its jagged edges and heavy-laden qualities, pain provides a reference point in a person's life, allowing one to appreciate what one has and who one is. Developing empathy would not be possible if a person were to never want for anything or experience hardships. And, of course, pain is a teacher; a person who burns a hand while cooking learns to be more careful with meal preparation.

> *Addictions.* Repetitive behaviors that become overpowering desires are addictions; examples include sexual obsession, alcoholism, and drug dependency. (Issues in Directives elaborates on these points on pages 143-146.)

> *Conventionalism.* The "common life" reveals a person's desire to be comfortable and content in everyday settings. This way of life—home and hearth—offers a sense of security, safety, and serenity. Routines are the order of the

day: work and household chores, marriage and family responsibilities, social gatherings, and community involvements. A life based on these values offers different things to different people but generally includes a preference for domestic living, interpersonal contacts, and regularities in one's comings and goings.

> *Peace and complacency.* One seeks an agreeable and accommodating life, valuing tranquility and harmony. The goal is to keep stress at a minimum by avoiding conflict and confrontation. Whenever possible, the person compromises with others and finds common ground, seeing aggression and argumentation as senseless and destructive. The downside, however, is that one may decide to not confront PSC simply because these conflicts would cause discomfort.

- *The prudential and the practical.*

  > *Judiciousness.* A person makes every effort to avoid exposure to potentially troublesome PSC. One may be watchful and restrained, cautious and calculating. While planning, anticipation, and thoughtfulness have their place, a person can become overly careful under the following conditions:

    o *Self-obsession.* Self-obsession may reflect a significant expansion of *pathos* with CTMI and emotionalism growing exponentially. Excessive concern with one's interests: "what's in it for me" and "me first" sentiments become dominant in the personality. The person lacks empathy and appears to only care for oneself.

    o *Playing it safe.* When aversive to risk-taking, the goal is to conserve and keep one's status and possessions safe. Fears involving failure, being ridiculed, and experiencing rejection are common motivators.

> *Pragmatism.* One takes a down-to-earth approach to is-sues, including solving complex, multifaceted enigmas. Pragmatism can be formal and businesslike, recognizing the time, energy, and resources required to achieve a goal. At its worst, the person is lacking in vision and an appre-ciation for the complexities of PSC and what lies ahead.

> *Fearfulness.* A person reacts to PSC with apprehension and alarm, even when no significant risk is involved.

> *Materialism.* Ownership of physical objects is highly val-ued. A need to purchase and possess an ever-increasing amount of "stuff" dominates the person's life. While living in a nice house with nice furniture may be desirable, the need for more can become an overwhelming and overrid-ing obsession.

> *Power and control.* An overriding desire to exercise au-thority over others by whatever means necessary is pres-ent; people are simply commodities having no intrinsic worth. Values involving excessive use of power and con-trol may develop during childhood in the following ways:

  o *The modeling effect.* The child identifies with aggres-sive and dominating parents, having witnessed their display of excessive control in the home.

  o *Obvious abuse.* Feelings of inadequacy caused by bla-tant abuse can result in the child developing similar abusive behaviors.

  o *Subtle mistreatment.* The child grows up in a seeming-ly ordinary household, but the parents subject him to subtle psychological mistreatment. The development of these same tendencies may result.

o *Direct teaching.* The parents teach the child that taking advantage of others is desirable. Aggression becomes the blueprint for social interactions.

> *Manipulation and exploitation.* Image-conscious and image-making individuals will utilize distortion, trickery, and lies in their interactions. Perhaps they are only trying to convey a strong message—pitch a product, a person, or an idea—but they could also be charlatans, con men, or liars. Manipulation can also occur from unconscious wants rather than deliberate deception. For example, one may use kind words and deeds to gain approval, acceptance, and adoration.

- *Ethics and moral reasoning.*

  > *Morality.* A person's sense of right and wrong usually develops over time but can also occur suddenly through an epiphany. Agreements and partnerships without a moral base eventually break apart. Developing and recognizing ethical standards requires an examination of the following issues:

    o *Individual differences.* People vary in their interpretation of moral behavior.

    o *Context.* The details of behaviors can completely change the moral implications.

    o *Culture.* Societal standards can vary significantly.

    o *Era.* Moral guidelines may develop and evolve depending on the time in which one lives.

    o *Relativity.* Taking the position that values are entirely fluid, interchangeable, and without definition, leaves the concept of moral reasoning vague and vaporous, with no accountability for a person's actions.

> *Humanism and altruism.* Examples include expressions of concern for others, acts of kindness, and involvement in organizations that help those in need. Additionally, one must consider both conscious or unconscious needs for control, power, or superiority and compulsive actions, as they may also factor into acts of charity.

> *Spirituality.* The "realm of the spirit" means less interest in what a person can physically hold and possess. A person may de-emphasize the buildings and rituals of conventional religion. Although identification with humanity, nature or even the universe may be present, the focus is on the intangible and the invisible.

> *Religiosity.* The practice of religion includes institutional membership practiced in a formal setting, with specific doctrines and dogmas, Scriptures, inspired books, and other sacred writings. Additionally, membership in a particular religion may also represent a commitment to one's ethnicity or community rather than necessarily a belief in its tenets. For many, religion provides a sense of belonging, security, peace, and fulfillment, in fellowship with like-minded believers.

> *Faithfulness.* Faith involves unquestioned belief and commitment, with two primary tenets: God exists, and God is good. Believing God is a continual presence in one's life can bring inner peace, serenity, and strength.

- *Standards.*

  > *Aesthetics.* A person holds beauty, fitness, form, and symmetry in high regard. Is the object, medium, or work attuned, balanced, and harmonic? A selection of standards to judge something as "fitting" or "appropriate" is considered essential, including flow, congruency, consonance, and compatibility. The arts, literature, music, nature, an-

imal and human form, and movement are illustrations of these values. An overemphasis on following a standard, however, can result in elitism and intolerance for any expression that does not conform to it.

> ➤ *Truth-telling.* A person seeks out objective standards in appraising "knowledge." Understandings involve logic, reason, scientific study, objective findings, detailed inquiry, and analysis. The search for truth generally follows either a scientific or philosophical investigation. Both attempt to define what is real and true, with critical thinking and objectivity respected above all else. A scientific approach requires rigor and methodology, while a philosophical treatise demands discipline and examination.
>
> Being honest is not simply whether or not one is deceitful. Although this is part of it, the truth can be distorted and compromised in many ways. Honesty requires understanding conscious, semiconscious, and unconscious motivations. Does a person meet reality head-on or choose to remain unfocused to avoid dealing with the issues? Without truth-telling, communications may disintegrate into manipulative tricks or expressions of unresolved CTMI. From a psychological point of view, deceptive practices come in two primary forms, including:
>
> o *The blocking of cognitive-emotional connections.* The unconscious process protects a person from fully experiencing the degree of pain radiating from pathos. Blocking and *pathos* complement each other; as *pathos* evolves, so do the blocking mechanisms. Almost simultaneously, spontaneously, and effortlessly, they become aligned, connected, and seamless. The blocking of cognitive-emotional connection's immediate impact is that one does not face insecurities, imperfections, torments, traumas, and conflicts. Furthermore, blocking has a secondary effect in

preventing a person from having a clear and complete view of reality; one does not learn life's lessons or profit from feedback. Unconscious TFA will leave one vulnerable and exposed. A person unaware of faults and shortcomings will further the blocking process. Central questions concerning the blocking phenomena include the following:

- ✓ *Consciousness.* To what degree are thoughts conscious or unconscious?

- ✓ *Purpose.* What are the underlying reasons for the blocking?

- ✓ *Extent.* What is the depth and breadth of the blocking?

- ✓ *Emotionalism.* What is the effect of overly emotional reactions on blocking?

o *The censoring and editing of TFA.* While blocking is unconscious, censoring and editing are usually conscious, with the deliberate intent to commit a falsehood. Consciousness, in this context, implies direct manipulations. A person "holds back" TFA, not overtly displaying intentions and making it difficult on others to follow one's line of thinking.

Censoring and editing occur principally when a person concludes there are adverse consequences to expressing specific TFA. One can be fired from a job, expelled from school, or sentenced to jail; one may become homeless and destitute, without family or friends. Censoring and editing are not the same, differing as follows:

- ✓ *Censoring* involves a person's active suppression of a TFA, whereby one does not sufficiently consider or reveal what may be objectionable. It is an attempt to keep secret, set aside, and hold back. Censoring includes the following types of interactions:

- *Avoidance.* Thinking through a potentially harmful interaction involving a PSC, weighing the pros and cons, and deciding not to get involved. This TFA is similar to suppression.

- *Aggression.* Bullying another person through physical or verbal intimidation, threatening actions, or hostile interactions. The strategy is to overwhelm, taking one off guard and instilling fear.

- *Excessive cautiousness.* Being overly careful, hesitating, or procrastinating. A pause, a wobbling, or a faltering happens because of fear. The person does not want to get into trouble and plays it safe, with the credo, "when in doubt, don't."

- *Withdrawal.* Becoming socially inhibited, primarily due to generalized anxiety. The person may be preoccupied with obsessions, compulsions, or addictions (OCA), leading one to pull back from social interactions.

✓ *Editing* involves the active altering, revising, correcting, changing, or expunging of a TFA. A person attempts to rewrite or rephrase a particular thought, feeling, or action, adjusting or rearranging it to change its status or meaning. Common editing strategies include the following:

- ◆ *Rationalization.* Avoid taking responsibility for one's actions by justifying, exaggerating, or minimizing one's role.

- ◆ *Intellectualization.* Bending and distorting facts but leaving enough resemblance to the truth that they may pass for the truth.

- ◆ *Compulsivity.* Repeated behaviors that are usually ritualistically performed to reduce anxiety or fear momentarily. Compulsive approaches reveal unresolved trust issues across PSC. The underlying motive is to rigidly adhere to a set schedule and standard in an attempt to be safe and avoid the risk that something could go wrong.

- *Connections.*

  - ‣ *Interpersonal relationships.* A person wants to satisfy the need for human contact through a variety of interactions, some meaningful and some not. Relationships with people, communities, and institutions are fundamental in life. Simply being around others can be intellectually and emotionally stimulating, occurring in many settings: places of worship, local VFW Halls, family parties and family reunions, sororities and fraternities, bowling leagues, friends at work, and the neighbors next door. But some people may avoid social interactions because they lack confidence or feel others may not support them. Excessive dependency may originate in a family setting, with parents and children over-relying on each other. One may also form excessive attachments to a community, organization, or government agency.

- *Seeking stimulation and sensation.*

  - ‣ *Vicarious living and spectator sports.* In the modern era, experiences through observing others are important to scores of people. Watching a  game and rooting for a favorite player can provide a welcomed distraction from the stresses of modern life, but it can become obsessive when a person over-identifies with teams or the players. Gaming is an additional example of vicarious living.

> *Media mania.* The desire to obsessively follow the news via print, TV or electronic devices often involves watching violence, protests, and uprisings. *Media mania* does not equate to staying informed with the news; it is another example of indirect living. One is attracted to something powerful, exciting, and possibly tragic that takes time, energy, thought, and feelings.

> *Risk-taking.* One's actions can expose a person to possible danger. Being bold and daring is exciting for these individuals as they participate in activities "for the thrill of it all." Risk-taking contrasts with *passion* (detailed on pages 135-136 to follow). A person pursues a goal with passion because of its significance, not primarily due to the intensity of the experience.

> *Antiauthoritarianism.* The need to rebel may initially form from parental figures who are intimidating and physically dominating, or subtle and psychologically manipulative. The person comes to feel that societal norms are artificial and excessive and wants to go against the system. One may initially embrace a conventional belief system only to reject it later. An example is a compliant and obedient child who becomes a rebel as an adult when new influences come into play. The nonconformist's mindset is to go "against the grain" and become a "rebel without a cause." Extreme examples, including gang affiliations, terrorist organizations, and criminal enterprises, often substitute for a family structure.

➤ *Attention-seeking and the prima donna complex.* The person wants to be noticed and preferably the center of attention. Petulant and demanding, one wants what one wants when one wants it. In the extreme, the person becomes obsessed with power and stature. Others may feel the need to "walk on eggshells" in the person's presence. Like the "emperor wears no clothes" anomaly, no one dares to speak the truth to this bully, who is subject to temper tantrums and ineffective leadership. Self-obsessions contribute to TFA in the following ways:

  o *Poor reality testing.* A fundamental understanding of human interactions and relationships is lacking. Empathy, respect, give-and-take, and common courtesy remain undeveloped when one does not profit from the feedback loop that social encounters offer. A person is too busy with one's own concerns and preoccupations.

  o *Problematic identity.* The person develops a disjointed and fragmented *PI*, leading to an expansion of *pathos*. One demands that treatment from others be "special," which may momentarily boost the person's self-confidence, but feelings of inferiority, anger, and resentment persist.

- *Passion*

  ➤ *Desire for intense relationships.* Wanting to love and be loved, a person strongly connects to another with empathy and a mutual coming together. Romantic, intimate, and committed relationships are examples. Some people also form deep bonds with their pets.

  ➤ *Commitment to a cause.* One develops an alliance with a movement based on intense principles and beliefs, which may or not be constructive.

> ➤ *Dedication to an institution.* A person embraces the purpose and meaning of an organization. Sacrifice and commitment are at the forefront; patriotism and military service are examples based on a sense of duty and obligation. However, one must be alert to extreme TFA developing due to such dedication.

> ➤ *Drive for intense involvement.* A person energetically and resolutely gives oneself over to a fervent pursuit. Obsessive-compulsive tendencies, however, may factor in and have a detrimental impact on a passionate inclination.

**Developing Directives**

A value system develops from participation in life events. PSC create emotional experiences and connections from which *directives* emerge. Initially, instincts and sensations are the driving force in the personality. Life steps in, compounding and possibly confusing what a person holds dear as values grow in number and complexity. Experiences, identifications, successes, and failures will have a significant influence, especially in one's early years. With the passage of time, relationships and involvements continually challenge a person's value system, altering it and, at times, turning it on its head. Unresolved discrepancies in *directives* caused by incompatible and contradictory values may persist, causing confusion in TFA.

The emotional power of the bonds formed with a person, institution, organization, or idea will impact values. The level of their intensity is what counts. For example, the relationship one has with a teacher or coach can powerfully affect the development of one's values, as can reading a deeply moving story. When the emotional connection is minimal, the identification process will not be robust, and values will not form. Beyond emotional intensity, several additional factors have a significant effect on the development of *directives*, including:

- *Balance. Directives* require balance to function efficiently; a person's life will spin out of control without it. The concept of balance is often misrepresented and misinterpreted, implying that it will compromise a person's individuality. Balance, however, preserves a person's integrity by preventing values from becoming extreme and overtaking the personality. A typical example of unbalanced *directives* is a person controlled by an addictive or obsessive-compulsive life pattern, leaving one's value system undeveloped. Or perhaps a person has abandoned one's values altogether to indulge in extreme behaviors. When values are balanced, the person will be more aware of these *directives*. Factors that influence balance include:

  > *Qualities and characteristics.* Balance does not mean that one's desires, goals, wants, and needs are similarly weighted. On both conscious and unconscious levels, a person gives a rating and ranking to one's values that can differ in the following ways:

    o *Diversity.* People are unique, fundamentally different, and distinct from one another. Balance does not suggest everything ends up in the middle—at the mean-medium-mode, muddled in mediocrity.

    o *Consistency.* Balance implies a degree of steadiness, consistency, stability, and composure.

    o *Flexibility.* Inventiveness and innovation are required when dealing with challenging PSC, often calling for radical and bold decision-making. While caution and carefulness are admirable traits, vacillation and wavering are not. Times and conditions may mandate that the person not walk a straight line because a "balanced" approach would be catastrophic.

    o *Emotionality.* The undercurrents of a person's motivations reveal balance's role in forming values. Is one acting from a place of balance—fairness, patience, and consideration? Or out of cowardice—hesitation, fear, and an unwillingness to take a stance? Intimidation and control, power and politics, and other outside influences and pressures may play critical roles in a person's emotional reactions to PSC, affecting the balance of values.

o *Knowledgeability.* Disregarding important factors can limit perspective and causes bias in one's understanding. A person's "balanced" approach to life could suggest one goes with what is easy and convenient, failing to explore some of the most relevant issues.

o *Observability and objectivity.* All aspects of PSC are constantly in flux. Reality testing is essential. Being ready and willing to change course at a moment's notice and embrace or abandon a balanced approach are crucial.

➤ *Underlying motivations.* "Finding balance" may also be used as an excuse to avoid making tough decisions. Motivational factors of this kind include:

o *Fear.* A person may "play it safe" because one is unsure and generally fearful. Regardless of the consequences of not taking action, the person avoids taking the necessary risks to resolve an issue, justifying the safe option by arguing that it is a balanced approach. Taking an overly cautious approach allows a person to evade repercussions from a bold and controversial decision.

o *Self-indulgence.* TFA outside the usual societal standards are not heroic if they are merely expressions of self-indulgence. Casting off civil behavior to satisfy hedonistic urges would not suggest one is brave and principled.

o *Something of significance.* Whether something is of such overriding importance that it outweighs the concept of balance remains a judgment call. Abandoning the safety of balance can be noble and inspiring, especially when a crisis requires action. A first-year medical student wanting to become a second-year student will need to lead an unbalanced life. Other examples may include 24-hour caregiving for a disabled person or working long hours to start a business. The same is true for a volunteer working in a foreign land, a soldier in a war-torn country, a doctor in residence on 24-hour call, a crisis intervention worker in difficult conditions, and a farmer getting his crops in before a killing frost arrives. These are examples of people foregoing balance to fulfill commitments to themselves or others.

> *Abandoning balance.* Although extreme TFA can be the product of noble efforts that lead to extraordinary achievements, one must always be aware of possible pitfalls when going down that path. Without balance, one's vulnerabilities can inadvertently replace a value system with obsessions, compulsions, or addictions (OCA). Possible problems associated with abandoning balance include:

o *Deep-seated compulsions.* Giving into continual urges can create an imbalance that may place a person on a self-destructive trajectory. Even when finding oneself in imminent danger, and calamity is about to strike, the person's compulsion controls one's behaviors; rational thought then plays no role in decision-making.

o *Complete moral bankruptcy.* A person will lose the sense of right and wrong without the guidance of a moral code. For example, when addiction becomes the priority, one may abandon ethical principles and embrace corrupt, unprincipled, and dishonorable behavior.

o *Self-destructiveness.* When survival and self-preservation instincts are lacking, watchfulness declines, and deficiencies in self-care, caution, and practicality occur. Reality testing is compromised, and the person gives little consideration to the potential consequences of one's behavior; self-control, stability, and careful study of PSC are absent. The losses may be catastrophic; family and friends, health and wealth, good name and reputation, house and home, profession and professional identity could all be at risk.

o *Excessive moralizing.* Preaching to others can also cause an imbalance in a person's value system. An example is a hypercritical person who views everything by its ethical implications. Quick to judge, one gives little consideration to the conditions surrounding an event, displaying only inflexible, orthodox, and unbending rigidity in relationships and understandings of PSC.

o *Perfectionism.* A person may be singularly devoted to the goal of making no mistakes, wanting to over-control PSC, along with heavy-handed criticism of oneself and others. This desire to be perfect can take over a person's TFA, creating a life without pleasure, joy, or self-care. The body may pay the price: stomach aches, headaches, fatigue, and exhaustion. Many roads may lead to perfectionism, with parents often playing a critical role in its development in the following ways:

✓ *Expectations.* Pressures on the child to think, feel, and act in specific ways can set into motion a child's desire to please the parents by striving toward unrealistic goals.

✓ *Overcompensation.* A child who has been repeatedly humiliated may react by developing perfectionistic traits.

✓ *Reaction and intense striving.* Perfectionistic tendencies of the parents may result in the child copying their behaviors. Or conversely, a lack of motivation in the parents' lives may bring about the child developing perfectionistic tendencies to compensate.

- *The elements of personality.* Directives are affected by *PI, II, CI, TI, pathos,* and *spiritus*, along with one's mental processing. At the same time, except for *spiritus*, personality elements and cognitions are impacted by *directives* in the following ways:

  ➤ *Imbalance and the creation of blind spots.* A person's values can result in an almost total lack of insight into oneself and the PSC that are encountered. For example, moral reasoning may play little or no part in one's life when a person values safety and security above all else. In another example, one's *PI* may atrophy in size, with *pathos* expanding into an aggressive, dominating entity. The person describes oneself as benevolent, caring, and even humanistic, but will stop at nothing to guarantee a position of authority and power. The effects of blocking, censoring, and editing are evident in both examples. When a person has blind spots, one can no longer see PSC objectively and dispassionately.

  ➤ *Domination of a particular value.* A single value can control a person's TFA, throw *directives* out of balance, and affect all of the elements of the personality.

  ➤ *Insufficient development of values.* When one or more of

a person's values are extreme, the other values needed for balance and growth are left undeveloped.

> ➤ *Rigidity of the value system.* A person's values may become locked in place, and adjustments sporadic, momentary, and perhaps meaningless. It then becomes less likely that one's *directives* will undergo significant change as time passes, affecting development across the personality.

- *Interests.* Sometimes curiosity and attraction to an object or activity may be the only motivating factors for continued involvement; no hidden meaning is present. Examples could include stamp and coin collecting, setting up a miniature town with a train running through it, playing golf or billiards, reading novels, going to movies, watching sporting events, baking a cake, and singing in the church choir. Interests, however, can also lead to compulsive acting out, as that which begins as a harmless distraction can take over a person's every TFA. A few hours a month becomes a few hours a week and then a few hours a day, eventually developing into a full-blown compulsion. When pastimes, hobbies, amusements, and avocations dominate a person's life, it is easy to lose one's way. Unconscious motivations may also contribute to the expanded and ingrained habit.

- *Extraneous forces.* When a person makes concessions because of political pressures, unwanted and unrealistic deadlines, or other stressors caused by PSC, one's values can become compromised or even vanish altogether. Accommodations and adaptations of *directives* crafted over a lifetime can cause a disjoining, inconsistency, and contradiction of one's values; the person no longer knows what truly matters. The following factors influence the strength and connection of a person's values to particular PSC:

> ➤ *Origin.* Understanding where one's values came from requires an examination of CTMI's role in their

development.

> *Quality.* Whether inherently positive or negative, values and their consequences need to be defined, along with their effects on TFA.

> *Consistency.* Confusion and disharmony among the values result in inconsistencies in TFA. Additionally, dealing with PSC's multidimensional issues is essential for a stable and understandable value system.

## Issues in Directives

A person's values can cross the line and become extreme—an expression of *pathos*, with one needing to look at the factors behind TFA. When obsessions, compulsions, and addictions (OCA) dominate a person, one has lost control of TFA. OCA each refers to specific behavioral patterns that significantly disrupt a person's value system. Obsessions and compulsions, often used interchangeably, are not the same. An obsession is a thought, and a compulsion is an act; they may or may not be connected. For example, when there is a direct connection between an obsessive thought and a compulsive action, it may seem as though the thought causes the action. While this is sometimes true, obsessions and compulsions can also act independently. Obsessions, compulsions, and addictions are further defined and delineated as follows:

• *Obsessions.* Obsessions are recurrent, repetitive thoughts, ideas, and themes. Emotions, conflicts, and values can fuel obsessions; fearing or wanting something to the extreme can completely override the ability to consider the consequences of one's actions. One could fear failure, intimacy, closeness, high places, bugs, germs, etc. Wants may also cause obsessive thoughts: owning an expensive sports car, passing the exam to get into college, or winning the lotto.

Obsessions are a matter of degree; a person may have strong desires but not be obsessed. Is the want, need, or fear so strong that there are no boundaries? Obsessions cause an imbalance in *directives* for the following reasons:

> *Drained-off energy resources.* Fewer emotional and intellectual resources are available to the person.

> *Consuming thoughts and images.* A compounding of negative emotional states is present.

> *Cluttered thoughts.* Focusing, synthesizing materials, and drawing conclusions become difficult.

> *Unresolved CTMI.* Deep-seated insecurities continue to interfere with all elements of the personality.

- *Compulsions.* Compulsions, or compulsive acts, involve repeated behaviors usually ritualistically performed. These actions may momentarily reduce the person's anxiety or fear. Compulsive rituals can become engrained, interfering with one's ability to function normally, and are problematic for the following reasons:

> *Trapped.* The person does not seem able to stop repetitive behaviors.

> *Consequences.* Compulsions are harmful when they continue for prolonged periods, causing one to lose freedom, focus, energy, resources, creativity, and perhaps empathy for others.

> *Losing control.* A particular want or fear can dominate *directives*; the compulsion becomes central to one's life, with other values put aside.

> *Work life.* Professional life will suffer because the ability to focus on the complexities of work is compromised.

> ➤ *Interpersonal relationships.* One's family interactions, friendships, and social life will deteriorate as the compulsion's demands increase.

- *Addictions.* Addictions can involve both thought and action. They are physical or psychological dependencies, presenting as cravings, needs, wants, and indulgences that have taken over the person's life. Endlessly repetitive by nature, one becomes entrapped with seemingly no way out. In a sense, *PI, II, CI,* and *TI* surrender to this acquired need, but paradoxically the addictions offer the person little joy. They persist even when one is acutely aware of the dangers and potential consequences of the addiction process. One's life can quickly spiral downward and become one-dimensional.

  Addictions sometimes develop as a reaction to a conventional and routine life. In the spirit of curiosity and adventure, a person may decide to try something new and exciting that offers temporary deliverance from everyday realities. The person unexpectedly becomes more entwined and encased in the addiction. Further compounding the problem, one may simultaneously have multiple addictions. Whatever the number, they are problematic for the following reasons:

  > ➤ *Unhealthy.* Addictions can cause a depletion of physical, intellectual, and emotional energies, with a person becoming fatigued, if not exhausted.

  > ➤ *Unfocused.* The person becomes absorbed into the addiction, influencing thinking as it decreases the concentration necessary for all cognitive processes. Integration and synthesis of thought, abstraction and conceptualization, comprehension, organization of materials, mental drive, creativity, and decision-making, all become impaired.

  > ➤ *Unconnected.* Relationships become meaningless and expendable. The person no longer values the qualities of a relationship—trust, honesty, communication, closeness

and intimacy, compassion, and empathy.

› *Unconscious.* With a lack of awareness, the addiction is more likely to become central to one's life, equivalent to a drive or a need. It may become an automatic response without thought, as the person loses control of the ability to consciously make choices.

# CHAPTER XIII QUESTIONS

1.  What are your most defining values?

2.  Do they seem to be changing?

3.  Do you compare yourself to others?

4.  Do you have a strong need to be in control?

5.  Do you have a solid sense of right and wrong?

6.  Do you have a need to be of service to others?

7.  Do you believe in God's continual presence in your life?

8.  Do you highly value the arts, literature, music, nature, form, and movement?

9.  Is telling the truth always necessary, or is "a little white lie" sometimes ok?

10. Are friendships important to you?

11. Are watching sporting events a top priority?

12. Is following the news important to you?

13. Do you seek out risky activities?

14. Do you like to show off?

15. Are you committed to learning new things?

16. Do you intensely connect with people, animals, nature, institutions, or ideas?

17. Do your values clash, or are they in agreement?

18. Can you make decisions if they are going to be unpopular?

19. Have you compromised your values due to outside pressures?

20. Do CTMI impact the values that you hold?

# XIV.
# SPIRITUS

In 1812, Jacob and Wilhelm Grimm published Grimms' Fairy Tales, a German collection of fables that includes the classic *Snow White and the Seven Dwarfs*. More than a century later, Walt Disney turned the tale into an animated film, adding to the folk story and renaming the dwarfs: Doc, Sneezy, Happy, Dopey, Bashful, Sleepy, and Grumpy. Doc is a wise but nervous leader and a problem-solver. Sneezy is friendly, loves to dance, and is unpredictable in his sneezing fits. Happy is cheerful and thinks everything is funny. Dopey is silly, fun-loving, and enjoys playing tricks. Bashful is shy and enjoys listening to stories. Sleepy always seems to be tired and perhaps lazy. And Grumpy complains and disagrees about everything but comes to the rescue of a friend in trouble. Each of the brothers has a unique way of being, seemingly unrelated to learning experiences. They appear to have come into the world with the essence of who they are; enter *spiritus*, the *sine qua non* of being, present from one's beginning.

## Defining Spiritus

*Spiritus* is the innate, innermost character and disposition present from the very beginnings of one's life. Words cannot easily define *spiritus*, as it answers to many names: spirit, soul, essence, and life force. Understanding the mind requires recognizing and accepting one's unique expression of *spiritus*, which is fundamental and essential to all TFA and present in every interaction with PSC. *Spiritus* becomes evident when one realizes that behavior is more than the product of thoughts and emotions created by early life experiences and the learning process.

Most of psychology's textbooks view TFA as reflections of a conditioning process that occurs from recent or long-ago experiences. These learnings are the product of early parent-child relationships, the Schools of Hard Knocks, books and teachers and mentors, playgrounds and streets, and trials and tribulations of everyday existence. But something is missing; as powerful as they are, the traditional theories leave one wanting more: a fuller explanation of the human drama. The concept of *spiritus* fills that gap and allows a more complete understanding of human nature. *Spiritus* is present before the ways of the world have a chance to take root. Every human being's foundation has an individual focus before life rushes in to further one's definition and development.

Life filters through *spiritus*; *spiritus* does not filter through life, since no events and experiences can alter a person's nature. Not merely the initial thrust into life, *spiritus* is a continuing influence on all to come. It is a prime factor and mover in determining each person's uniqueness. While *PI, II, CI, TI, pathos,* and *directives* combine with intellect to account for nearly all of the descriptive terminology used to define "mind," *spiritus* also needs to be part of the mix. Meanwhile, traditional science also leaves questions unanswered by reducing *spiritus* to the genetic code and biological influences. One day scientists will accurately spell out the human genome—the genetic blueprint. But even with this accomplished, *spiritus*'s nature and etiology will remain a mystery.

**Subtypes of Spiritus**

No list of words can describe the qualities or characteristics of *spiritus*; the possibilities are endless. *Spiritus* consists of those innate and particular features that each person possesses. *Spiritus* expresses itself in countless ways, reflected in the uniqueness of thoughts, feelings, and actions (TFA).

## Developing Spiritus

*Spiritus*, fundamental and essential to all TFA, is present in a person's every PSC interaction. *Spiritus* does not go through a developmental process. In a sense, it is pervasive and eternal, while the other elements of the personality are earth bound and transient. Because *spiritus* predates the intellect and the personality itself, it is not initially part of consciousness. *Spiritus* is separate and distinct from identifications, learnings, or even thought, although it continually influences all of these functions. So, while all the elements of the mind are affected by *spiritus, spiritus* is not affected by them; the relationship is a one-way street. As a person develops, one may readily grasp the influences of *PI, II, CI, TI, pathos, directives*, and the cognitive processes because they reveal themselves directly in interactions with PSC. But *spiritus* can only be recognized and understood through self-exploration, acknowledged and accepted as the underlying "wonder child"—innocent, primal, elemental, and foundational.

Understanding *spiritus* is to know that people do not reduce to biological robots, as evident by contrasting the creative capacity of the mind with the logical discourse of the machines. Although easily outperforming humans with greater accuracy, efficiency, and productivity in most tasks that require strictly cognitive functioning, computer systems do not equate with the mind. Through the millenniums, humankind's astonishing achievements, both in beauty and scope, are far beyond the reach of technology's nuts and bolts. *Spiritus* gives the thinking processes an original and singular comprehension that computers do not possess.

## Issues in Spiritus

*Spiritus* is everywhere and nowhere. Everything flows through *spiritus*, and *spiritus* affects everything in the process. Is *spiritus* an element of the personality? The answer is no and yes. While it is not a part of a person's developmental history or the result of a learning process, *spiritus* is wholly entwined with and has a pervasive effect on all aspects of the personality. Although *spiritus* communicates primarily through the unconscious, it may also speak plainly and simply on a conscious level, allowing one to grasp its meaning and intent. TFA may be in step with *spiritus*, or consciously and unconsciously react against it. Generally speaking, *spiritus* affects the other elements of personality in the following ways:

- *PI. Spiritus* influences *PI* by guiding a person in specific directions, affecting one's experiences and understanding of them. *Spiritus* and *PI* may or may not mirror each other. For example, one's *spiritus* might be reserved and hesitant, with a person reacting to these restraints with a bold and brash *PI*. Or a curious and exploratory *spiritus* may be reinforced with a person's *PI* developing into an adventurous world traveler. *Spiritus* and environmental presses create unique life experiences that influence *PI*.

- *II. Spiritus* strongly influences who a person engages and who one avoids. Relationships have mystery, symmetry, and alchemy; a person may be drawn to or repelled by the inherent and unconscious associations of the *spiritus* of another. These interactions may be consistent with one's *spiritus* or entirely in opposition, but either affects a person's identity. Social encounters become a self-reinforcing process: *spiritus* influences relationships and establishes the connection between *II* and *spiritus*. An example of compatible connections is when a person's *spiritus* is aggressive and drawn to combative people, creating a threatening and contentious *II*. In contrast, an illustration of an opposite association is a highly reserved *spiritus* causing one to link up with friendly and engaging people, resulting in *II* becoming more expressive and socially appropriate. Interactions, then, may be highly consistent with *spiritus*, completely the opposite, or not connected at all.

- *CI. Spiritus* and *CI* may reflect or contradict each other. *Spiritus* affects a person's attraction to a wide array of groups. An example showing commonality is an outgoing *spiritus* and a *CI* active in community affairs. An opposite example has a person's *spiritus* reserved, but *CI* connects to unrestrained organizations.

- *TI. Spiritus* may affect the way a person views the non-material side of reality. A person whose natural tendency is objective, logical, and scientific may or may not develop a *TI*. But one whose *spiritus* is intrinsically interested in religious studies is likely to be drawn to the transpersonal.

- *Pathos.* Understanding the unconscious connection between *spiritus* and *pathos* is essential to comprehending this unique relationship. Even when *pathos* is not the primary result of *spiritus, spiritus* influences *pathos.* While the learning process from CTMI commonly plays a dominant role in creating *pathos, spiritus* also impacts it when opportunities arise. For example, when *spiritus* is stable and subdued, it could have a quieting effect on the qualities of *pathos* that develop over the years, perhaps allowing a person to overcome destructive TFA. However, if *spiritus* tends to be aggressive and agitated, it could increase *pathos*'s intensity.

- *Directives.* The wants, needs, and desires of *spiritus* may influence *directives* by favoring specific values and having little interest in others. For example, the relationship is complementary when both emphasize safety or orient to venturous behaviors. In contrast, conflict occurs when one may lean toward security and the other toward riskier pursuits.

Because *spiritus* is already present from the beginning, it powerfully impacts both the personality structure and cognitive processes. More than any other factor influencing the mind, it defines and distinguishes a person; *spiritus* is the most significant determiner of individual qualities. But it is not one's destiny, as that is the product of all the elements of personality and the intellect. By accepting *spiritus*, a person may find ways to accent and build on inherent strengths while compensating for intrinsic weaknesses. Betraying *spiritus* by denying unique characteristics impedes the forces that propel a person forward. Acknowledging and understanding *spiritus* is challenging because it is not the product of CTMI or other life experiences. Yet because it is the most significant influence on the development of the other elements of the mind, becoming aware of its impact on one's life could not be more vital.

# CHAPTER XIV QUESTIONS

1. What natural tendencies have you always noticed about yourself?

2. Do you have distinct qualities that do not seem to be connected to your upbringing?

3. Do they seem unrelated to learning experiences?

4. Is there a deep sense of who you are beyond the roles you play in the world?

5. Have you reacted positively or negatively to others for no apparent reason?

6. Do you sometimes wonder why you are involved in particular pursuits and activities?

7. Do you have spiritual pursuits beyond your family background and religious teachings?

8. Do you have personal issues you cannot explain?

9. Do you have values that seem to have always been there?

# The Process of Thought

# XV.
# INTELLECT

Is a human being smarter than a field mouse? The answer is not a simple yes because it depends on what one means by the word "smarter." Unlike the field mouse, humans can solve math problems, write poetry, remember important dates, and learn a foreign language. But our furry little friends display an acute and penetrating intelligence in adapting to challenging and complex environments. One can only grasp the role of intellect in the functioning of the mind by taking a multidimensional perspective.

## Defining Intellect

The intellect is a composite of interconnecting and interacting cognitive operations, akin to a computer processing mounds of data and drawing conclusions. It consists of thinking processes that are not separate and distinct because many of them require several cognitions working simultaneously. This chapter primarily focuses on gaining an understanding of cognitive functions alone. The role of personality, and its impact on intellectual functioning, will be addressed in the chapter to follow, Cognitive-Personality Connections.

## Subtypes of Intellect

While intellectual abilities overlap and intermix, their essential characteristics include the following:

- *Mental drive.* The source of energy through which cognitive processes flow that is the product of one's physiology and personality. The degree to which one is awake and alert affects the desire to learn and explore avenues of thought.

- *Initial listening.* When the mind is able to fully engage and "lock in" with minimal distraction when first exposed to a challenge. It is essential to understanding the information from the beginning as one lays the groundwork for determining the next step. Furthermore, giving one's full attention shows respect to a person, an institution, and the content itself.

- *Sustained attention.* Continual focus necessary for memory to form. One must become and stay fully engaged to avoid distractions. Whether they are exciting or dull, distractions compromise a person's attention. Distractions can be external interruptions or occur internally when the mind takes flights of imagination or struggles with emotional concerns. And while creative endeavors have their place, they can interfere with the task at hand and detract from one's focus. Personality correlates can also have an impact, with impatience and impulsiveness in particular detrimentally affecting sustained attention.

- *Memory.* While forms of memory functioning share some common elements, they also have the following unique properties:

  ➤ *Short-term memory.* Holding knowledge for a brief amount of time.

  ➤ *Long-term memory.* Recalling information after a significant amount of time has passed.

  ➤ *Systematic memory.* Basing recall on logical or organized associations as in remembering stories.

  ➤ *Rote memory.* Using repetition to recall materials with no logical connections, like a series of numbers.

  ➤ *Visual-spatial memory.* The ability to recall shapes, sizes, angles, locations, and movements.

> *Personal memories.* Recalling friendships, family relationships, successes and failures, and other past events and experiences.

- *Logical thought.* To reason and use dispassionate analysis. Logical thinking involves abstraction and conceptualization, synthesis of materials, and problem-solving.

  > *Abstraction.* Generalizations made by drawing materials together. The distilling of characteristics reduces data to a set of essential features; it guides a person in constructing hypotheses and theories.

  > *Conceptualization.* A higher level of abstraction involving mapping out specific elements and their relationships.

  > *Synthesis of materials.* An in-depth review of issues allowing one to make the necessary connections, combining concepts and information into coherent wholes.

  > *Problem-solving.* The careful study of variables, including those not obviously connected. This cognition requires initial theorizing about these factors and ruling out alternative explanations. Not only must the raw data be studied and understood, but one needs to know about the people involved and their role in solving the problems.

- *Objectification or realism.* The act of making PSC quantifiable, observable, external, embodied, and concrete. Objectification is similar to logic in that it requires a clear understanding of the present condition with a realistic appraisal and approach to PSC. As a result, the person can experience PSC beyond the theoretical, abstract, and "idea" of something and make them into something present, visceral, and tangible.

- *Practical reasoning.* To stay grounded by not losing sight of the basics and recognize the most critical issues in everyday functioning by using:

➤ *Common sense.* Being aware of what is obvious, clear, and evident.

➤ *Pragmatism.* Keeping things simple and responding to the basic needs of a problem.

- *Coherence.* Being connected, unified, and congruent in thought, word, and deed. Messages are understandable, consistent, and consonant with each other; thinking is not scattered but has direction and clarity.

- *Organization.* Systematically and methodically arranging ideas and reasonings that require self-discipline and strategizing, planning and preparation. Chaotic thoughts are difficult to follow; ideas need to be clear and precise, including an analysis of PSC.

- *Simplification.* To reduce redundancy, confusion, and unnecessary complications. When something becomes too complex, people tend to tune out altogether. Simplify does not mean shrinking the materials to the point they lose their essence, but reducing complicated ideas in the following ways:

  ➤ *Details need to spell out the subject matter.* Conceptual underpinnings are understandable when detailed information illustrates the meaning behind any theoretical presentation.

  ➤ *Speak and write plainly.* Communicating in common, familiar, everyday terms and minimizing overly technical words and phrases make things more understandable.

  ➤ *Reduce information overload.* Information pervades society and overloads with its confusions, contradictions, and irrelevancies. Data overwhelms people and the institutions they represent with reports, bulletins, and news items. Knowledge is only powerful when it is accurate and significant. Making sense of data and evaluating its worth requires one to examine distinctive characteristics of information and ask the following questions:

 o *Source.* Does the information come from a reliable and trustworthy authority with a record that has proven itself over time?

 o *Objectivity.* What are the undertones and motivations? Are there inherent preferences, tendencies, and prejudices? Has there been a deliberate attempt to deceive or manipulate the information?

 o *Methodologies.* How are sources of information gathered, data analyzed, conclusions drawn, and reports written?

 o *Relevance.* Is the investigation being reported pertinent and applicable to the current topic?

 o *Representation.* Was a study chosen primarily due to its consistency with a person's orientation?

- *Attention to detail.* Recognizing the importance of carefully spelling out concrete, undeniable information. Attending to detail involves steady and methodical "detective work"—carefully gathering relevant information and avoiding excessive and unnecessary generalizations. The information must be sufficient to support one's position but not so detailed that the deeper understanding is lost.

- *Intuition.* An impression or sense about PSC. A person develops an awareness from hunches and is able to distinguish intuitions from emotions. Over time one becomes more comfortable trusting this form of knowing.

- *Openness.* With maturity, patience, and perseverance, becoming open to new experiences and allowing one to develop:

 ‣ *Objectivity.* Responding without bias to PSC.

> ➤ *Flexibility.* Displaying a willingness to make adjustments in TFA.

> ➤ *Optimism.* Seeing the possibilities.

- *Perception.* The ability to form impressions of PSC accurately. Perceptions involve acute recognition and insight in the following areas:

  > ➤ *Social awareness and social intelligence.* Assessing PSC, including developing a critical understanding of the conscious and unconscious motivating forces behind people and institutions. Social intelligence involves learning to read PSC and intentionality; becoming a keen observer of the dynamics between and among people is critical. The subtleties of human communications include attention to the following:

    o *Social cues.*

    o *Speech patterns.*

    o *Slips of the tongue, insinuendoes.*

    o *Body movements, including arm and leg movements and the use of the hands.*

    o *Facial expressions, including frowns, smiles and rolling of the eyes.*

    o *Head movements, including shaking of the head and nodding in agreement.*

  > ➤ *Anticipation.* To foresee possible problems and proactively take the necessary precautions to prevent them from happening. Even when no apparent difficulties are present, one needs to stay attuned to issues that may prove to be of critical importance.

- *Multidimensional thinking.* To be able to hold multiple ideas in one's mind. Reflexive and imaginative thought processes involve switching from one cognitive set to another. Ideas that appear not to be connected may be vital to understanding the phenomena under study and require one to address the following issues:

> *Nexus points.* Explore the possible connections among issues, the focal points that bind the concepts together.

> *Going beyond the obvious.* Be willing to take unpopular positions with minimal support from others.

> *Consideration of other options and ideas.* Explore other possibilities from a wide array of sources, including seemingly unlikely and possibly extreme views.

• *Inspired and original thought.* A state in which vision and imagination breathe life into an idea. Some of the ingredients for originality include the following:

> *To not prejudge.* Allow for the flow of thoughts through the mind, uncensored and open to new ideas, feelings, and impressions.

> *Finding common ground.* When working with others, mutual understanding and integration of thoughts create esprit de corps.

> *Acquiring knowledge.* Depending on the complexity of the subject matter, it may be necessary to develop both depth and breadth of the phenomena under study.

> *Stepping away and re-evaluating.* Examine the underlying assumptions one has taken.

• *Holism.* An overarching view, understanding the long-term implications of problem areas and the decision-making process. It is the theoretical framework a person utilizes, the meaning and significance behind the phenomenon, and going beyond the details and specifics. One considers the grand schemes and intents, with their philosophical underpinnings to expand understanding. While this conceptual approach shapes information into a coherent whole, if the focus is only on the "big picture," one could miss essential details. Furthermore, when attempting to achieve a holistic vision, fanaticism becomes a possibility. Radical positions can move farther and faster than logic or reason, leading to a cult-like following and a mesmerizing fascination for those involved. Paradoxically, when one must face a toxic and damaging PSC, there may be little choice but to respond with fiery intensity and enduring commitment to overcome those negative influencing factors.

## Developing Intellect

The home environment, life experiences, and academic opportunities are the most significant influences on cognitive development. Additionally, everyday stressors can strongly impact intellectual advancement and maturation, with inner and outer turmoil and distractions compromising a person's ability to learn, process information, and make decisions. For these abilities to develop, a person needs to be challenged and grow in the areas previously outlined in Subtypes of Intellect.

## Issues in Intellect

What is the relationship between instincts and the intellect? Are instincts unlearned and biological, fixed behavioral patterns to specific stimuli, or perhaps simply hunches, impulses, or a sense about PSC? Although often unconscious, instincts can offer unique insights that affect major life decisions. Contrasting instinctual to analytical approaches provides an opportunity to understand their distinct ways of recognizing and resolving issues concerning oneself and the world:

- *Grasping PSC's significance.* Instinctive is intuitive and insightful, while analytic is investigative and fact-finding.

- *Problem-solving.* Instinctive is free-spirited and spontaneous, while analytic is contained and orderly.

- *Confrontations.* Instinctive is self-confident, self-assured, and bold, while analytic is reserved and careful.

- *Self-definition.* Instinctive is uncritical, while analytic is self-reflective.

- *Understanding phenomena.* Instinctive is attuned to bodily sensations, while analytic is logical and reasoned.

- *Risk-taking.* Instinctive is daring and open to new experiences, while analytic is cautious and calculating.

# CHAPTER XV QUESTIONS

1. Do you feel mentally awake and alert most of the time?

2. Are you easily distracted?

3. Can you keep track of things?

4. Are you able to think through complex issues?

5. Are you realistic in appraising PSC?

6. Can you sift through mountains of details and maintain a focus on what is most important?

7. Are you consistent in the messages you give out?

8. Are you able to present your ideas so others can understand them?

9. Do you pay enough attention to the details of an issue?

10. Do you trust your instincts in solving problems?

11. Are you able to spot the motivating forces behind someone's actions?

12. Can you hold many thoughts in your head to solve complex problems?

13. Do you consider the long-term implications of an issue?

# XVI.
# COGNITIVE-PERSONALITY
# CONNECTIONS

Comedian Groucho Marx once quipped, "I sent the club a wire stating, PLEASE ACCEPT MY RESIGNATION. I DON'T WANT TO BELONG TO ANY CLUB THAT WILL ACCEPT ME AS A MEMBER." Groucho's joke makes the point that feelings can override logic when making decisions. In a continual dance, the structure of thought and the elements of personality form connections that determine one's perception and experience of people, situations, and circumstances.

## Defining Cognitive-Personality Connections

Personality and cognition continually interact and influence each other. They connect in two main ways: the moment-to-moment thinking process and one's attitude toward thinking and acquiring knowledge. A person may be unaware of these instantaneous and intertwined happenings that react to each other, becoming a single unit in the process. Even when a problem is straightforward, ordinary, and familiar, personality variables affect one's thoughts, for better or for worse. Feelings flowing through personality also influence a person's access to cognitive functions. The reverse is also true: cognition affects personality. A person's ability to gather, categorize, analyze, and summarize information impacts emotional functioning and how one responds to PSC.

**Subtypes of Cognitive-Personality Connections**

Vulnerabilities in the elements of personality can result in confusion and even incoherent thinking. Asking the following questions can help to uncover the cognitive-personality connections (CPC) that create blind spots in one's understanding of PSC:

- *Identity.* Do the characteristics and interactive effects of *PI, II, CI,* and *TI* create an identity that is stable, consistent, and harmonious? Do identifications foster a rational and reasonable view of people and institutions?

- *Pathos.* To what degree are CTMI and emotionalism affected by continuously over-thinking or re-thinking PSC, replaying recent or long-ago events? How frequently does one review unpleasant experiences or have thoughts of regret over lost opportunities?

- *Directives.* Are values out of balance? One or two values may completely dominate a person, as when obsessions, compulsions, and addictions take control and create areas of vulnerability. (see Chapter XIII, Directives, for a complete description of blocking, censoring, and editing) The person's thinking becomes unidimensional and cloudy because one cannot see beyond the envelopment, affecting cognition through:

  > *The blocking of cognitive-emotional connections.* Blocking occurs when one does not want to deal with the difficulties of PSC in everyday life encounters. Blocking provides temporary relief from internalized stress, but the cost of this reprieve is high—a denial or misinterpretation of reality.

  > *The censoring and editing of thoughts, feelings, and actions.* A person develops a cognitive approach that avoids difficult issues and denies a role in their creation, especially when the problems are long-standing. It involves

deception and impairs one's ability to develop cognitive strategies.

## Developing Cognitive-Personality Connections

CPC form when the inner workings of the personality and the external world of people, situations, and circumstances (PSC) combine to affect a person's development and functioning. When CPC are not a problem, a person performs well in personal and interpersonal endeavors. The significant influences on this interplay include the following:

- *Stressors.* The common distressing and sometimes disabling conditions impacting personality and the thinking process include:
  - ➤ *Physical and mental fatigue.*
  - ➤ *Physical, mental, and emotional discomfort and pain.*
  - ➤ *Noise and distracting sounds.*
  - ➤ *Unpleasant people, situations, and circumstances.*
  - ➤ *Job pressures.*
  - ➤ *Financial difficulties.*
  - ➤ *Sleep deprivation.*
  - ➤ *Poor general state of health and well-being.*
- *Emotional reactions.* All emotions can compromise or enhance cognitive functioning. In particular, the following features of emotionality (extreme and grossly inappropriate emotional responses) can negatively impact focus, judgment, synthesizing, and decision-making:

➤ *Over-reactivity.* Internal or external emotional responses—expressed or kept inside—leading to instability.

➤ *Low frustration tolerance.* Diminished patience in dealing with the complexities of PSC.

➤ *Lack of empathy.* An inability to relate to the experiences of others causing impairment in understanding PSC and a breakdown in relationships.

• *Awareness.* A person's ability to step out of and objectify one's thinking will enhance cognitive functioning by:

➤ *Recognizing reality.* Acknowledging one's TFA in responses to PSC. Intellect and personality come to understand the outer world from different frames of reference and may completely disagree in assessing PSC's relevance and significance. These internal disputes resolve more easily when others validate one's experiences.

➤ *Calmness.* Setting aside internal and external distractions.

➤ *Learning of strengths and weaknesses.* Understanding one's intellectual and emotional gifts and liabilities, including unique abilities, competencies, and deficiencies.

➤ *Reviewing personal biases.* Becoming aware of the generalizations one forms about PSC revealed through tendencies, inclinations, and leanings.

• *Capacities.* While some actions or acquired skills qualify as automations, others are a direct product of the personality and influence cognitive abilities. Capacities may show strengths and deficiencies in the following areas:

➤ *Communications.*

o *Social interactions.* Understanding the nuances of working collaboratively with others.

o *Vocalizations.* Expressing oneself clearly and persuasively.

> *Skill sets.*

o *Problem-solving.* Using logic, organizational thought, attention to detail, practical reasoning, intuition, perception, and multidimensional thinking.

o *Focus and concentration.* Avoiding distractions, confusions, and contradictions.

o *Time management.* Spending an appropriate amount of time and energy on materials. When excessive information is available, reviews of documents can be endless and may result in incidental, irrelevant, or erroneous conclusions. Two personality factors may contribute to the repetitive and redundant reviewing of materials:

✓ *Unnecessary caution.* Fear of making mistakes and the consequences should they be discovered.

✓ *Extreme worry.* A tendency to ruminate over irrelevant issues.

> *Intellectual self-discipline.* A commitment to learning, thinking, and problem-solving. One is willing to toil over tedious and detailed materials that are challenging and complicated. Intellectual discipline includes:

o *Preparation.* Developing steadfastness, drive, and energy to learn something well and master it. The sheer amount of information can overwhelm a person, affecting the ability to focus, remember, analyze, synthesize, and learn.

o *Patience.* Making an effort to determine what is

worthwhile, insignificant, or simply wrong.

o *Decisiveness.* Knowing when the time for pausing and reflecting is over and choosing a course of action has arrived.

o *Steadfast in approach.* Managing daily obligations and duties.

➤ *Knowledge.*

o *Acquisition.* The process of gaining information.

o *Organization.* The method utilized in arranging and retrieving information.

o *Conceptualization.* The significance and implications of acquired knowledge leading to the formation of a concept.

o *Storage.* Keeping and making information readily available.

➤ *Learnings.*

o *Life experiences.* Ordinary learning acquired as one goes through everyday routines.

o *Formal schooling.* Academic learning required to gain expertise in a field of study.

o *Informal settings.* "Street smarts" acquired through exposure to life's challenges, including the development of acute understandings of PSC.

o *The mentoring process.* Direct learning that takes place through face-to-face interactions and affiliations. The depth of these relationships can profoundly affect one's understanding of PSC.

## Issues in Cognitive-Personality Connections

A person's outlook and embraced beliefs create attitudes and traits that affect CPC. A trait exists when a person generalizes across all PSC. An attitude, in contrast, is directed and focused, categorizing only specific areas of one's experiences. A trait is like an attitude gone wild, becoming all-encompassing. Whether an attitude or trait is "good" or "bad" depends on one's assessment of the particulars of PSC. Generally, they give the person unique insights and understandings when dealing with an array of life events. A lack of attitudes and traits indicates a person has no opinions, ideas, views, or formulations and has not learned from experiences and challenges with PSC. Attitudes potentially provide a strategy for mapping out PSC. However, if one lacks objectivity and overgeneralizes, the attitude has become a trait that may lead to misinterpretations of PSC.

Pessimism, negativity, and optimism are attitudes or traits that can be unstoppable forces, becoming more powerful than a person's intelligence, education, background, finances, creativity, or special abilities. Forms of pessimism include suspicion, mistrust, and an expectation of the worst outcome. Discouragement and disappointment, if not despair, may then dominate TFA. A negative view of people and possibilities is similar to pessimism, as it emphasizes faultfinding and complaining, opposition and invalidation, contrariness and disapproval. On the brighter side, an optimistic view of people and possibilities—combined with a good dose of realism—offers a sense of encouragement and enthusiasm to the person and those with whom one interacts. This outlook provides a surge in energy, allowing the elements of personality and cognition to work well together. Goals that appeared unattainable may now feel within reach.

# CHAPTER XVI QUESTIONS

1. How does stress affect your ability to communicate clearly and effectively?

2.  How do your emotional reactions impact your decisions?

3. How do feelings affect your thoughts?

4. How do thoughts affect your feelings?

5. How do stressful PSC affect your problem-solving, concentration, and productivity?

6. Do emotions get in the way of learning?

7. Do you see yourself as optimistic or pessimistic?

8. Can you put thinking ahead of feelings when necessary?

# XVII.
# OPTIMAL THINKING

In his biography, Nikola Tesla recalled that as a child, he was excited when he saw a steel engraving of Niagara Falls and "pictured in my imagination a big wheel run by the Falls." Tesla viewed the Falls as a stunning display of nature's unlimited force and as a way to harness energy. He told his uncle that he would someday "go to America and carry out this scheme." This dream became a reality in 1895 when The Niagara Falls Commission chose General Electric's polyphase AC (alternating current) system, advanced by Tesla, to create the first hydroelectric plant, changing the way the world used electricity. He profoundly impacted life on the planet by blending curiosity, imagination, and reasoning capacities.

## Defining Optimal Thinking

Optimal thinking (OT) is cognitive functioning at its peak; the brain is "firing on all cylinders." One processes information with little wasted energy in solving enigmatic and multifaceted problems. Optimal thinking occurs when all aspects of intellectual functioning—focused attention, logic, objectification, coherence, organization, vision, simplification, and flexibility of thought—work in harmony.

## Subtypes of Optimal Thinking

Automations and habitual thought patterns influence optimal thinking, for better or for worse, in the following ways:

- *Automations.* A series of conditioned responses that are typically not intentional, calculated, or conscious but repeated so often that they become mechanical. TFA become almost robotic. Initially, automations are not automatic but involve thinking, perhaps even planning.  But after many repetitions, some TFA simply happen because they have been happening. Routines of everyday living can quickly become automations because no pondering or struggling through a problem is needed. Values play a minimal role in these TFA since they are typically not willful or self-directed. Automations are not aspects of the personality—*PI, II, CI, TI, pathos, directives,* and *spiritus*—or the intellect. Examples include washing the dishes, cutting the grass, taking a shower, and feeding the dog. They do not involve blocking out the negativity of *pathos*, with its undercurrents of CTMI and emotionalism. Automations are both helpful and harmful to the development of optimal thinking:

➤ *Why they are good.* Potentially, automations save time and energy. They allow a person to complete multiple routine tasks simultaneously; an example is talking on the phone while making coffee.

➤ *Why they are problematic.* Because deliberate thought is not involved in automations, one is more likely to make mistakes. Being excessively on autopilot can decrease problem-solving and decision-making skills because a person is less likely to consider the complexities involved or the consequences of actions. The following proactive practices can minimize their interference with optimal thinking:

  o *Periodic "check-ins."* Realize the qualities of PSC have different and distinct features; it may be necessary to go through one's actions step by step.

  o *Refocusing.* Review the problems and the people involved in an interaction.

o *Acceptance of change.* Recognize that the conditions in which one lives are not constant, immutable, or permanent; stay alert to the fluidity around PSC.

o *Acknowledgment of mistakes.* When a mistake becomes apparent, make adjustments to prevent its reoccurrence.

o *Awareness of complacency.* Realize one's actions can become careless and sloppy even when things are seemingly going according to plan. In those moments, a person may not pay attention to the nuances of PSC. Keep automations in check to avoid missing the signs of a developing problem and take necessary precautions or preventative measures.

- *Habits, current impact.* A series of conditioned responses, but unlike automations, can be the product of associations formed on a conscious or unconscious plane. Examples include eating rituals, academic routines, and work schedules. Habits that affect one's ability to think through issues include:

  > *First thoughts and first actions.* One initially has ideas, "first thoughts" about involvements with particular PSC that lead to an immediate response, "first actions," which may be reasonable or impulsive and could even be reckless. These "first thoughts" persist and may become ingrained, so when similar encounters with PSC occur, a linkage rapidly forms with the "first actions." The impact of this pattern of behavior depends on the wisdom behind the initial development of the connection.

  > *Fantasizing.* For most people, taking journeys of the imagination is a common practice. The benefits of this kind of thinking may include a creative burst of energy with fresh ideas and images that offer unique insights. Fantasizing can also be relaxing by removing the person from

the stressors of the day. But when it becomes habitual, the following changes in TFA can occur:

- o *Unrealistic beliefs concerning life's complexities.* The complexities of PSC are compromised because of a failure to appreciate the practical implications of one's actions.

- o *Disallowance and denial of realistic concerns.* Abandoning logic, deductive reasoning, and the synthesis of information can lead to poor judgment because one ignores critical details and facts concerning PSC.

- • *Habits, long-term impact.* Giving up established routines may cause unforeseen problems. A person may become caught up in the attraction and intrigue of entirely new ventures. The departure from traditional standards has its place; innovative ideas that initially seem unusual may bear fruit at a later point. Desiring and pursuing change that disrupts usual practices, however, can result in the following negative consequences:

  - ‣ *A lack of focus.* Diversions draw a person's attention away from current activities, affecting performance on the tasks at hand.

  - ‣ *Inadequate planning.* Overlooking the preparation and organization of current responsibilities, the person repeatedly makes mistakes.

  - ‣ *Abandoning current involvements.* Unexpected desertion or neglect of the usual operations may cause confusion, chaos, and a demoralizing effect on others.

  - ‣ *The compounding effect on other pursuits.* Too many ideas at one time can result in a person not carefully thinking through one's actions.

> *Diverse interests.* Outside attractions draw in some people and turn off others, disrupting a spirit of cooperation.

> *Manipulations to take the advantage.* Another person or institution may use the promise of involvement in new ventures to manipulate PSC.

> *Limited reflection on feelings and thoughts.* When one hurries through routines because of the lure of something new, unexpected consequences often happen.

## Developing Optimal Thinking

Optimal thinking (OT) occurs when the elements of personality are in sync, distractions are minimal, and stimulation is not too much or too little, as follows:

- *Personality Structure.* Personality and cognition are intertwined, acting as one dynamic force. A person can enhance the development of OT by addressing these questions:

  > *PI, II, CI, and TI.* Do significant discrepancies and disharmony exist among the forms of identity? Are confusion and contradiction present in the person's identity?

  > *Pathos.* Are significant unresolved conflicts, traumas, and malevolent identifications (CTMI) operating, resulting in deep-seated insecurities and hostilities? Does intellect play a minimal role in decision-making due to the dominance of emotionalism in the personality?

  > *Directives.* Has a dampening of awareness by blocking cognitive-emotional connections or censoring and editing of thoughts, feelings, and actions occurred? Have obsessions, compulsions, and addictions become so dominant as to overwhelm the person and the thinking processes?

Is the person's value system out of balance, lacking accommodation, modification, and clarification?

> ➤ *Spiritus.* Is there a fundamental lack of understanding and acceptance of one's nature, resulting in inappropriate reactions to PSC?

- *Distractions.* Coming in all sizes and shapes, they are anything that limits or affects a person's train of thought, causing focus to no longer be sharp. An array of feelings may enter in and color a person's perceptions and experiences, possibly distorting understanding PSC. Not all of them are a nuisance, as some are a breath of fresh air—stimulating, tantalizing, exciting, or simply fun. But even pleasant interruptions draw a person away from the task at hand by disrupting the flow of concentration. Perhaps a person is bored, stressed, or worried, hoping for a diversion from something that is bothersome. Suddenly, focus is no longer sharp or defined, and one may even believe that the deflection is "the answer" to these problems and worries. But the person is ignoring the present tasks because diversions on the outside have made their way inside. For example, a person hears a dog barking, and momentarily, the sound captures one's attention, and focus lessens. The intrusions might also bring up memories, associations, and emotions, further diminishing attention.

  Distractions, however, may not only be desirable but necessary. Sometimes, a person may need to remove oneself from a specific task to keep the flow of thought, and the diversion serves that purpose. Enthusiasm and vigor may result from a "break in the action," with a renewed freshness and inventiveness in one's approach.

- *Stress.* Stimulation can be a blessing or a curse, depending on its intensity and duration. Optimal thinking requires optimal stimulation, which is individually determined. What some experience as anxiety, others relish as exciting, if not exhilarating.

Beyond a certain point, provocations and incitements are experienced as stressful, disruptive, and unsettling; they interfere with OT. The pressures are real, and people have visceral reactions to them.

The person's ability to understand PSC can go beyond thinking when conscious, semiconscious, and unconscious thought processes work together. When functioning at its zenith, optimal thinking creates a flow state. Fully immersed in an activity, difficulties become effortless, and surroundings fade into nothing. A flow state, however, will not be permanent and may suddenly vanish. But for some period of time, a person functions at maximum capacity regardless of PSC's intrusive or disruptive qualities. Being in a flow state and *striving toward clearmind (CM)* are bound together. Like flow, *CM* involves personality elements—*PI, II, CI, TI, pathos, directives,* and *spiritus*— and cognitive processes working as one unit.

Distractions seem to evaporate as hyperawareness of the focal point of one's activity comes to the forefront. Extreme sensitivity and awareness allow a person to separate what is essential from what is irrelevant. Emotionalism is put to the side, allowing a person to conserve and channel energies. One demonstrates detachment and dispassion, avoiding reactive, sensational, and histrionic responses. A flow of energy is released and propels a person to go beyond the usual level of performance.

A deeper, instinctive, and unconscious form of *CM* is evident when one is in a state of flow. The person may almost appear to be in a trance, bypassing the laborious process of step-by-step thinking through an issue. Subconscious thinking becomes a source of integration, and the mind brings ideas and knowledge into focus. Influencing variables include:

- *Beginnings.* The stars align: the person has experienced a *state of CM*, is confident in his ability to attain a particular goal, and TFA are in a harmonic rhythm.

- *Endings.* When *CM* fades away, this heightened, supercharged experience will almost immediately dissolve, offering no guarantee that it will return.

- *Strength and durability.* Being in this state does not necessarily mean a person is unstoppable and superhuman. Sometimes one's performance is not out-of-this-world but still quite remarkable. Depending on one's level of *CM*, confidence, and rhythmic TFA set in motion, this flow state may be brief, or last for an indeterminate length of time.

- *Pragmatic concerns.* Flow state does not always result in positive outcomes. Being high on success can result in one becoming inattentive and careless, with errors in judgment that bring the flow state quickly to an end. A person performing effortlessly and flawlessly may become overconfident, believing one can do no wrong, not having taken the time to go through the arduous process of looking ahead to consider what comes next.

## Issues in Optimal Thinking

Beyond purely cognitive abilities (see Chapter XV, Intellect), a person's attitude toward and understanding of PSC enhances optimal thinking in the following ways:

- *Attitude.* Taking a constructive approach to challenges with positive self-talk helps one focus and avoid negative internal programming of *PI, II, CI, TI, pathos,* and *directives.* Optimistic thinking aids a person in maintaining a realistic perspective, regardless of the stress level. Curiosity—a quest for knowledge fostered by an overwhelming desire to learn—can help one's striving toward OT, energizing the sense of wonder in anticipating new ventures to explore.

- *Understanding.* Being savvy, smart, and possibly shrewd in dealing with people and institutions are part of OT and includes developing and utilizing the following skills:

> *Perception.* The ability to see clearly through images and appearances, remaining alert to others' motivations.

> *Active listening.* To focus on the details of the communication, avoiding internal and external distractions.

> *Attuned to tactics and controlling maneuvers.* Being aware of the strategies often used to persuade others. Different types of these schemes include:

  o *Character assassination.* The expression "If you throw enough mud at a person, some of it will stick" is the tactic of repeatedly accusing someone of something malicious and harmful.

  o *Twisting the facts.* Distorting the facts while retaining some elements of the truth, includes willful contortions designed to discredit a person, a position, an institution, or an idea.

  o *Dire consequences.* Repercussions are often used as threats if a person does not follow another's dictates.

  o *The good-ole-boy network.* Those in positions of power make decisions, while those most affected are unaware of the discussions.

  o *Bully-boy tactics.* Forcefully making oneself known pressures others to conform.

  o *Feeding the bias.* Reinforcing populist notions, leanings, and preferences employs both subtle and flagrant manipulation.

> *Caution to not misinterpret communications.* Taking care to realize that not everything reduces to trickery and

deceptive practices. Communications may be misleading or confusing due to others' deficiencies in knowledge, verbal skills, organization abilities, or general level of intelligence.

# CHAPTER XVII QUESTIONS

1. What daily routines occur without thinking about them?

2. Does multitasking work for you?

3. Do you tend to think through your actions step by step?

4. Do you find it helpful to review problem areas in your life?

5. Are you willing to admit your mistakes?

6. Do you take precautions as soon as you spot a potential problem?

7. Can you let go of a particular approach when it's not working?

8. Are you, at times, not practical or realistic enough in dealing with PSC?

9. Do personal conflicts impact your ability to make sound decisions?

10. Do obsessions, compulsions, or addictions play a part in your life?

11. Are you easily distracted?

12. When do you become fully immersed in an activity?

13. Do you occasionally become overconfident, and if so, what is the impact?

14. Does positive self-talk boost your confidence and sense of well-being?

15. Do you find it helpful to study people and their communications?

# XVIII.
# SHARPNESS

During the preliminary phase of a homicide investigation, iconic television figure Lt. Frank Columbo tells the person he suspects of murder: "You know, sir, it's a funny thing. All my life, I kept running into smart people. I don't mean smart like you or the rest of the people in this house. You know what I mean. In school, there were a lot of smarter kids. And when I first joined the force, they had some very clever people there. And I could tell right away that it wouldn't be easy making detective as long as they were around. But I figured if I worked harder than they did, put in more time, read the books, kept my eyes open, maybe I could make it happen. And I did. And I really love my job, sir."

Suspects misjudge Columbo's ability to elicit information, and one by one, they fall into his traps. After completing an interview, he heads toward the door but abruptly turns back because he has "just one more thing" to ask. Suddenly and unexpectedly delivered, this last question catches the suspect off guard and unnerves him. The murderers realize all too late that they have woefully underestimated this seemingly simple man with messy hair in a rumpled trench coat and lost the game of cat and mouse. Columbo's overly polite manner and somewhat fumbling approach deceive the criminals. Being able to piece together bits and pieces of seemingly unrelated information that destroy their alibis and reveal their motives captures the characteristics, subtleties, and effectiveness of being sharp. The usefulness of this particular skill set is not limited to detective work but may prove invaluable as one encounters challenging people in a wide variety of situations and circumstances.

**Defining Sharpness**

While standard cognitive processing can help with understanding issues across the spectrum of PSC, comprehending and managing complex PSC require more. Being sharp is difficult to define because it is more than vocabulary, memory, calculating, reasoning, and other cognitive functions, as measured by traditional assessments of intelligence (IQ tests). Sharpness is a specific form of intelligence that allows one to see the intricacies of complex and confounding challenges and become aware of the broad spectrum of motivating forces behind TFA. At times, it calls for one to be crafty, cunning, and calculating, keeping a person from becoming victimized by the schemes and tricks of con artists, swindlers, and scoundrels. A cornerstone of clear and decisive action, this form of thinking offers acute insights into PSC that are farsighted and penetrating.

**Subtypes of Sharpness**

Sharpness expresses itself in three ways:

- *Intuition.* A piercing and nearly instantaneous understanding of PSC based on personal experiences and encounters, intuition is the purest form of sharpness, with an acute focus on the subject matter and exceptional perceptiveness that seems like the work of a prophet or seer.

- *Examination of the data.* Using a systematic, organized, and highly structured approach to grasp the underpinnings of PSC, an appreciation of the complexities of issues allows for predicting the troubles that lie ahead.

- *Analytical comprehension.* With less emphasis on gathering background information, an understanding is reached by blending deductive reasoning and anticipation.

Usually, a person with sharpness combines and merges all three forms, using one more than another at different times to gain an understanding of PSC and resolve complex problems.

**Developing Sharpness**

When one is exposed to a broad spectrum of people in an array of situations and circumstances, the following qualities of sharpness emerge:

- *Attuned to motivations.* Acutely aware of *directives*, one asks: What do others want and need?

- *Hardened.* Tested and educated in the School of Hard Knocks, a person learns to fend for oneself under trying conditions, developing resilience in all spheres of life. By enduring failure, disappointment, and discouragement, one becomes smarter, stronger, and wiser.

- *Balanced in values.* When a person's *directives* are aligned and balanced, one can avoid developing obsessions, compulsions, and addictions (OCA) that would detract from the ability to quickly assess another's thoughts, feelings, and actions (TFA).

- *Sensitized to nuances.* A person grasps PSC's distinctive and idiosyncratic elements in determining which responses will be most effective at any moment in time.

**Issues in Sharpness**

Balancing the following factors create a keen understanding of PSC:

- *Planning and strategizing.* At its best, sharpness allows a person to look ahead and make adjustments. Still, plans can go astray, causing complications, unnecessary troubles, and compromising the development of sharpness in the following ways:

> ➤ *Micromanaging.* Excessive control and obsessive-compulsive approaches to problem-solving can result in stress for all concerned, especially in a work environment. Because micromanagers lack trust in others' abilities, people tend to be on edge in their presence. Sharpness requires curtailing this tendency to overcontrol, allowing one to foresee its personal and interpersonal impact.

> ➤ *Over-planning.* Extreme preparation compromises sharpness as the individual becomes unimaginative, rigidly adhering to a preset plan. When told to follow an exact script, creativity is likely to diminish. Especially when facing danger and unpredictability, one may be unwilling to take a chance. Spontaneity and improvisation vanish, along with the courage to be innovative. Answering the following questions can help one avoid these pitfalls to sharpness:

>> o *Is there inflexibility?* A person needs to adjust his approach to complicated problems only to the degree that warrants it, keeping room for improvisation or alternative actions.

>> o *Is the approach excessive?* Planning can be overly detailed and stifling when there are mountains of petty details to consider; it becomes nearly impossible to sort through the information in a timely fashion.

- *Independence.* To maximize sharpness, one must decisively and confidently take positions guided by principles and a set of ideas about how the world works.

- *Emotional stability.* Feelings play a role in affecting perception on conscious and unconscious levels. The following aspects of emotionalism—extreme emotional reactions—interfere with sharpness:

> *Impulsiveness.* Hasty and careless, reacting without considering the consequences of one's actions.

> *Dramatics.* Histrionic, theatrical, and emotionally extreme, striving to be noticed, accepted, and rewarded.

> *Selfishness.* Narcissistic, self-indulgent, and self-centered, lacking empathy, concern, and care for others.

> *Hostility.* Arrogance and antagonism that may come from CTMI and emotionalism, or simply reflect manipulative strategies, including intimidation, coercion, or scare tactics.

> *Anxiety and panic.* Uncertainty and uneasiness to minor stressors.

> *Social inhibitions.* Difficulty being assertive and forthcoming, with a fear of not living up to expectations that causes one to avoid PSC that could result in failure, disappointment, or rejection.

> *Dependency.* An excessive need to be taken care of by others.

> *Obsessive-compulsive tendencies.* Hypercritical and judgmental, with a need for order and control.

- *Reality-testing.* Sharpness requires a practical, objective approach to understanding and engaging PSC. The following TFA detract from developing this ability:

> *Ambiguity.* Expressing oneself in an unintelligible and non-transparent way.

> *Disorganization.* An unsystematic approach to PSC.

> *Uninformed.* Relying on inaccurate and unreliable

information.

> ➤ *Rigidity.* An emphasis on order and control of PSC that can cause confusion and chaos.

> ➤ *Impracticality.* Idealistic and naive, lacking an understanding of the ways in which things work in the everyday world.

- *Interpersonal awareness.* Sharpness requires understanding people's interactions beyond words, including body language. One must recognize the undertones and subtleties that are not openly expressed in the communications.

# CHAPTER XVIII QUESTIONS

1. What are some of the ways you go about understanding and dealing with PSC?

2. Are you attuned to people's possible motivations?

3. What experiences have helped you develop resilience in the face of difficult PSC?

4. Is being in control of PSC highly important?

5. What preparations do you make when faced with a challenging task?

6. What guides your approach when dealing with difficult and complex problems?

7. When is it difficult for you to figure out what a person is up to?

8. What subtleties of a person's behaviors and communications do you pay attention to in attempting to get to the bottom of things?

9. What interferes with your ability to understand and deal with problematic PSC in a practical and objective way?

10. What interpersonal skills are most helpful to you in understanding others?

# XIX.
# STRATEGIC PHILOSOPHY

The innocence of childhood is not a permanent place of residence but only a temporary lodging to nourish the soul. A person must then strike out on one's own and find a place in the world. Harsh realities await; one cannot get by with just a smile. A person realizes that something else is needed: a *strategic philosophy (SP)*, a way of seeing the world to predict how people and institutions will act and react across the spectrum of situations and circumstances. At its best, *SP* embodies the wisdom of the ages by merging penetrating insights, emotional connections, and a balanced value system in one's approach to life.

## Defining Strategic Philosophy

*SP* is a belief system that every human being creates, designed to predict how people and institutions act and react. It is a serious inquiry serving as a guide to help one navigate everyday life and avoid its dangers and difficulties. Often involving careful study and introspection, *SP* forms when a person reflects on experiences, strengths and weaknesses, successes and failures. When functioning at peak performance, it is a penetrating probe into the meaning of life. But *SP* can also be primitive, crude, destructive, and self-destructive when it involves little or no thought process. Although this "road map" develops naturally, it does not necessarily get a person where he wants to go but sometimes leads to chaos and confusion.

*SP* is not a one-size-fits-all philosophy nor a cookbook approach to navigating the vast array of PSC one must face. It is an individualized plan to help sort things out and guide future choices and actions. It is usually not permanently fixed early in life but continually changes and expands. Through a process of discovery and invention, evaluation and evolution, each person uniquely crafts a personalized *SP* in attempting to get from "here to there."

*SP* requires the questioning of life's journey. Do things happen randomly, with nothing to do about it, or can one's daily life be understood and coped with to a reasonable degree of predictability or probability in understanding PSC, or at least possibilities to explore in adapting to them?

*SP* is intuitive by nature; consciously and unconsciously, one creates a survival manual to navigate life's choppy waters. It is not intrinsically good or bad, wise or witless, practical or fool hearty, although, in hindsight, it may seem to have all these characteristics. It is not a moral code of conduct, even though elements of one may be present. When facing overwhelming challenges, *SP* potentially enables a person to outwit and outlast an adversary by doing whatever it takes to survive and, when required, even becoming wily and scheming, plotting and calculating, slick and smooth.

**Subtypes of Strategic Philosophy**

*SP* includes the theories that a person develops "about how things are" and "about how things will be." One may be unable to predict a person's behaviors based on his *SP* because other influences may be more decisive and override them. But a person's *SP* can still reveal what one is likely to do with the usual conditions of life when there are no dire consequences for one's actions.

Understanding *SP* requires the following considerations:

- *Conscious and unconscious factors. SP* is the person's own study of "truth," as opposed to absolute or universal truths, a "best guess" of future encounters with PSC. As unreliable as one's beliefs about PSC often are, a person will still adopt them with both conscious and unconscious levels of awareness as follows:

  ➤ *Conscious processes. SP* will primarily be conscious if

a person, generally speaking, is aware of his TFA. Consciousness involves active planning and analysis of the issues surrounding PSC; however, it does not assure that *SP* is developed and mature. Censoring and editing, which are mostly conscious, involve manipulation and deceit to protect a person from compromise and concessions.

➤ *Unconscious processes.* When a person lacks awareness, *SP* will also result in a corresponding lack of control of TFA. However, the unconscious is not only the blocking of cognitive-emotional connections; it consists of many functions. Among them is the vast storing of understandings and wisdom, potentially allowing *SP* to function at a high level when under its influence.

• *Distinguishing SP from directives.* Values are broader and deeper than one's *SP*. A person's *SP* may be as simple as a proclamation, whereas *directives* involve the entire spectrum of the value system. *SP* may include aspects of *directives*, but at best, it is only a partial synthesis of the knowledge and understandings one has accumulated since childhood. *Directives* potentially represent the blending and balancing of all of a person's wants and wishes, needs and desires, fantasies and ideals, while *SP* focuses on one's understanding of PSC. *SP* and *directives* are mostly independent of one another. However, if they are in sharp contrast, confusion and inconsistency in TFA will occur because it will be unclear what the person stands for, and decision-making capacities will diminish.

## Developing Strategic Philosophy

Even in those first years of life, a person begins to generalize about people and institutions. These hypotheses are confirmed or contradicted with the passing of years based on repeated experiences, expectations, analytic abilities, and beliefs. *SP* can develop as a person painstakingly reviews personal history of both pleasant and unpleasant experiences and looks for recurring patterns. With the spectrum of philosophies one could embrace, from *survival of the fittest* to *the story of the Good Samaritan*, developing an effective *SP* requires ongoing reflection and introspection.

The degree to which *SP* continuously evolves varies for each person. It is set early in life for some people—perhaps as soon as the age of 10—but for others, *SP* will continue to adjust and adapt throughout their lives. While *SP* as a firmly established "completed project" in childhood has limitations, it is not desirable for it to still be changing at age 100. Fostering *SP*'s development requires the following:

- *Knowledge*. *SP* cannot expand and develop without a strong desire to understand people, institutions, situations, and circumstances. This knowledge is acquired and distilled directly and indirectly.

- *Life Experience*. A person cannot develop *SP* if one chooses to avoid life's challenges. Regardless of the degree of pain or disappointment they may bring, daily trials and tribulations provide the spark that nourishes *SP*.

## Issues in Strategic Philosophy

*SP* uses a general proposition about how things happen. But the unpredictability and uncertainty of the world mean that the best-laid plans do not always work out the way one intends. Back-up planning involving alternate approaches to problematic PSC is often needed. Depending on the particulars, a person needs to recognize when to make exceptions to guiding principles. As *SP* becomes more defined with each experience—step-by-step, back-and-forth, side-to-side, up-and-down—a person is less likely to reject it, even in the face of irrefutable proof to the contrary. When one has committed to a particular belief system and a "blind eye" effect results in a reluctance to give it up, objectivity may be lost or compromised. Since life consists of twists and turns, uncertainties and misgivings, and doubts and fears, outcomes will sometimes be disappointing. When confronted with contradictory information, a person may rationalize one's actions, becoming defensive, agitated, and unwilling to moderate positions. Rather than actions coming from a productive and inspired life plan, this rigidity often results in poor decision-making.

While *SP* requires flexibility due to PSC being in constant motion, grounding is also needed. The waxing and waning of one's viewpoints create uncertainty and a lack of clarity in thinking. This continual shifting of one's positions demonstrates a lack of a genuine set of beliefs; the person has not thought through the entire spectrum of issues regarding people, institutions, and organizations. TFA become inconsistent and perhaps even reveal a frivolous attitude; one's line of discourse lacks credibility. When a person shifts one's stance too easily and quickly without considering PSC's complexities, the following factors may be in play:

- *Intellectual laziness.* A lack of interest or energy in thinking through issues, or simply being unaware of the facts.

- *Gullibility.* Not taking or holding positions, believing that all truths—if they represent anything—are malleable and open to interpretation. A contrary stance may easily persuade a person who has not reflected on the issues.

- *Emotionalism resulting in dependency.* A tendency to shift positions to gain approval from others.

- *Emotionalism resulting in rebellion.* Being dominated by emotions and taking the opposite stance, seemingly regardless of the issues. The person is antiauthoritarian, angry, and rebellious, looking for someone to "take on."

In addition to rigidity and a lack of grounding, other factors contributing to errors in the construction of *SP* include:

- *Inaccurate conceptualizations.* Mistaken ideas about people, institutions, and society that lead to faulty understanding and ultimately unsound decision-making.

- *Unresolved personality correlates. PI, II, CI, TI, pathos,* and *directives* that distort *SP* due to a lack of development and integration among the personality elements.

- *Motivational mishaps.* Not thinking through PSC, but carelessly and hastily making decisions based on intellectual miscalculation or emotional dysfunction, resulting in a life without planning and strategizing. If a person's *SP*'s formation and design are haphazard and whimsical, modern society will prove challenging and likely overwhelming.

- *Extremism.* TFA that are self-destructive and significantly outside of standard actions and reactions. But there are exceptions; the specifics of PSC may deem "extreme" reactions necessary. For example, within totalitarian regimes, one may have little choice but to act outside conventional norms.

- *Psychological issues.* A diminished ability to develop a coherent and consistent philosophy due to the following dysfunctions:

    ➤ *Cognitive.* Impaired intellectual functioning usually involving poor comprehension and diminished deductive reasoning.

    ➤ *Emotional.* Maladjustments in the elements of the personality, including the person's identity and value system. Examples include severe depression, chronic anxiety, rage reactions, and panic attacks.

    ➤ *Poor reality testing.* Symptoms of psychosis that include delusions, hallucinations, and a lack of orientation, preventing the person from thinking through even the simplest of plans.

# CHAPTER XIX QUESTIONS

1. What strategies do you use to deal with PSC?

2. Do you question how things are going and realize when they are not going well?

3. What makes it especially difficult for you to handle PSC?

4. What adaptations and accommodations do you make so things go smoother?

5. How has your understanding of people changed over the years?

6. How do you approach difficult situations and circumstances?

7. What have been some of your most challenging experiences, including ones that have not gone well?

8. Have you developed backup tactics to deal with particularly problematic PSC?

The Rhythm of Life

# XX.
# PERSONALITY CONSTRUCTS

Throughout human history, across the vistas, cultures, and centuries, one sees complexity, confusion, and contradiction at every turn. Sometimes people's actions do not fit even their self-defined images; they engage in behaviors that appear contrary to the interests of themselves and others. Thoughts may be bizarre and erratic, emotions extreme and volatile, and actions dangerous and destructive. Others will observe that people abruptly change, with a lack of consistency and stability occurring across people, situations, and circumstances (PSC). How is one to explain these perplexities of human thoughts, feelings, and actions (TFA)? The answer lies in the realization that people do not have one all-encompassing personality but rather possess multiple *personality constructs (PCs)*—free-standing and self-contained units of personality.

### Defining Personality Constructs

Why not have just one big personality? Because it is the nature of the identification process (see Chapter II) to create an army of little personalities, an assemblage of discrete, detached, and disconnected *PCs* that may work with or against each other. *PCs* come into being one by one and usually have little in common. Mostly they are fragmented, with some of the elements of personality—*PI, II, CI, TI, pathos,* or *directives*—missing. It is the particulars of the identification process that determine the makeup of each *PC*. Over time, as more identifications take root, a myriad of them form. Multiple and diverse *PCs* are the norm, not the exception, for all human beings. Mostly, a person is unaware of the conflicts, contradictions, and complexities existing among the vast expanse of *PCs*. Although the identifications that create *PCs* may be conscious or semiconscious, they tend to be unconscious.

The combined forces of people, situations, and circumstances (PSC), along with *spiritus*, emotional and physical conditions, and awareness, result in the activation of specific *PCs* in the following ways:

- *PSC*. Regardless of whether the pressures of life are an entirely internal affair or externally produced, they affect the energy flowing into *PCs*. Continuous stress drains a person's intellectual, emotional, and physical resources, resulting in more reactive *PCs*; acute stress could fuel specific *PCs*.

- *Spiritus*. This guiding force within the personality is not a part of *PCs* but profoundly affects them. It is a one-way street; *spiritus* influences *PCs*, but *PCs* do not influence *spiritus*. Because *spiritus* is unique and particular to each person, no generalizations about its positive or negative impact on *PCs* are possible.

- *Emotions*. *PCs* are more consistent and reality-based when over-reactions are not present. The potential for immature and ineffective behaviors increases under the following conditions:

  > *Temperamental reactions*. When TFA are fleeting, merely passing through, a person may quickly, nearly automatically switch to another *PC*. A more extreme and possibly abnormal personality emerges. Temperamental reactions exaggerate a person's TFA and are frequently associated with anger, outbursts, and even rage.

  > *Emotionalism*. As an enduring part of the personality that represents a feature of *pathos*, emotionalism in *PCs* intensifies temperamental reactions. With emotional instability already present, initial reactions can immediately escalate from slight irritation or frustration to full-blown panic, rage, or sobbing.

- *Physical condition*. When one has chronic pain and bodily discomfort, inconsistency in the functioning of *PCs* likely occurs.

- *Awareness.* Being cognizant of the specifics of one's *PCs* de-creases their unpredictability. Understanding their similarities and differences—and the inconsistencies and incongruencies among the *PCs*—allows a person to guide his TFA in a coherent and meaningful way.

## Developing Personality Constructs

A person's unique internal processing of PSC designs and composes each *PC*. They do not develop uniformly but emerge and interact in the following ways:

- *Command.* With so many individual constructs being created, a *central PC* with authority over other *PCs* forms. It develops when intense identification with someone or something strongly influences the person. Connections between the central *PC* and other *PCs* may be consistent and cohesive or conflicting and disjointed. Multiple *central PCs* may also exist when two or more are central and of approximately equal influence, even though dissimilar from each other. Each *central PC* will connect to the spectrum of *PCs* in different ways and degrees, affecting a person's understanding of PSC. Thoughts may then become splintered as one's actions continually waffle back and forth, displaying inconsistency and indecisiveness.

- *Stability.* Often when *PCs* initially form, they are similar and compatible with one another, but these relationships continually change and evolve, for better or for worse. *PCs* compare and compete, establishing a pecking order that determines which ones will rule the roost. So regardless of their initial compatibility, *PCs* will ultimately react against one another and create more instability.

- *Adjustments.* Connections between particular *PCs* and PSC may cause some of them to change their level of importance relative to others. *PCs* can become too dissimilar to work together harmoniously. As they then become contrary to one another, inconsistent TFA occur.

- *The sheer number*. With each passing day, the proliferation of *PCs* and the conflicting identifications that create them increase the possibility for more splits and separations in the personality. Too many "mini personalities" emerge, causing uncertainty and confusion in understanding oneself and others.

- *Uniqueness*. Each *PC* has its own set of characteristics based on a person's identifications. One or more of the elements of personality—*PI, II, CI, TI, pathos,* and *directives*—is likely to be absent from a *PC*, with some having only a single element. This imbalance can cause extreme TFA, especially when *pathos* is the sole element of a *PC*.

- *Connections*. The similarity and intensity of one's experiences affect the development of the *PCs* and the consistency of behaviors. Since the connections among *PCs* are usually contrary and contradictory, TFA can become even more incongruent as they continue to proliferate and diversify.

- *Strength*. The power of a *PC* depends on the characteristics of the initial identification and subsequent reinforcements. A strong emotional connection can make a *PC* inflexible and decrease one's openness to new ideas. But a *PC* resulting from a significantly weaker identification process can be problematic in the opposite direction, with little or no level of consistency or integration with other *PCs*.

- *Clarity*. *PCs* that form under confusing and stressful conditions are usually poorly developed, fragmented, and lacking transparency.

## Subtypes of Personality Constructs

Unlimited combinations of highly distinct *PCs* potentially exist, with multiple variations possible depending on the identification process that brings them into existence.

## Issues in Personality Constructs

Grasping the nature of *PCs* is essential in one's attempt to understand when a person's conduct is "out of character"—erratic, peculiar, strange, or even bizarre. A conventional analysis of human behavior cannot make sense of these inconsistencies caused by variations in the composition and configuration of a person's *PCs*. When *PCs* are dissimilar and lack communication, connection, and integration, the potential for this "out of character" phenomenon increases. As a person "flips" to a *PC* not seen before, others may be surprised: "Oh, what got into him?" or "I've never seen him like that!" When a person switches, perhaps instantaneously to a different *PC*, it seems like an alternate personality has taken possession. The mild-mannered quiet person becomes explosive and out-of-control; the prudent, cautious conservative becomes a go-for-broke risk-taker.

What happened? Rapid and radical changes in mood, temperament, and personality are set in motion by issues—triggers—that are especially sensitive for a person. Usually unconscious and the result of a conditioning process, triggers are individualized emotional sensitivities that cause an exaggerated response. They develop throughout one's lifetime and often without awareness. Even a person's thoughts or worries can cause an overreaction. Triggers originating in childhood are more problematic because they tend to be unconscious, and reasoning capabilities are less developed. Also, with the passing of years, these early triggers are now deeply ingrained into the personality. Unbeknownst to observers and often the person, they may activate an extreme *PC*.

These *PCs* that stand out because they are significantly at odds with the others are called *outliers*. While all *PCs* have conscious and unconscious elements, the *outlier* is primarily unconscious. Its singularity among *PCs* makes it unique, a "stand-alone" that is the product of a particular identification process, often involving trauma and forming early in life. As the person ages, the *outlier PC* grows further apart and becomes more distinct from the other *PCs*, which are themselves becoming established. Connections between the *outlier* and the other *PCs* may break down altogether. When conditions similar to those that created the *outlier* reoccur, it again takes center stage. PSC need not be identical but only similar to the original conditions that caused the *PC* to activate the *outlier*.

An example of this phenomenon is an adult who hated and feared an abusive father during the childhood years but, nonetheless, formed a strong identification with him. With the activation of the *outlier*, the now adult takes on his father's characteristics. When the trigger recedes into the background, the person's more usual ways of behaving returns. But since the *outlier* is present in the person—albeit unconsciously—a similar PSC can easily switch it back on again. Sometimes an *outlier* can form from a positive rather than negative identification. For example, a child who felt neglected by the parents but unconditionally loved by a grandparent may develop an *outlier* that is exceptionally nurturing, a quality inconsistent with the now adult's usual demeanor but triggered at different times and conditions.

# CHAPTER XX QUESTIONS

1. Who have you formed strong emotional connections with at different times in your life?

2. How have these identifications impacted your TFA?

3. Do you seem to have very different or even opposing traits and personal characteristics?

4. How do you explain these similarities and differences in your personality?

5. Do you, at times, seem to be going in opposite directions?

6. Do you, at times, find it difficult to understand yourself and others?

7. Do you have personality quirks that you find hard to explain?

8. Is your behavior sometimes out of character?

9. Do you have emotional flareups, sometimes set off by little provocation?

10. What gets to you and sets you off?

# XXI.
# THE CLOUDING OVER OF MIND:
# FEARS, INSECURITIES, & INHIBITIONS

Dense fog rolls into Old London Town. The enveloping haze makes it difficult to find one's way to the local pub where friends await. Even though a person can hardly see one's hand, it is well worth the journey through the cobblestone streets to reach a place where one can relax and unwind. Likewise, finding one's way through fears, insecurities, and inhibitions (FII) can lead to being at ease with oneself and the world.

### Defining Fears, Insecurities, and Inhibitions

Fears, insecurities, and inhibitions (FII) can come from stressors in the environment, or they can form entirely in the imagination. They have value in life's drama by alerting a person to potential dangers and difficulties with PSC. But FII become problematic when they are expressions of *pathos*, flowing out of conflicts, traumas, and malevolent identifications (CTMI). Operating on conscious, semiconscious, and unconscious levels of awareness, FII can further compound and compromise a person's TFA, decreasing the ability to make sound decisions in everyday life. As a form of emotionalism, FII can be far-reaching and overwhelm a person's *central personality construct (PC)*, with other *PCs* following its lead. While fears, insecurities, and inhibitions are interrelated, they distinguish themselves in the following ways:

- *Fears.* Someone or something is upsetting. Fears are reactions to PSC and may or may not be a realistic assessment of dangers. Regardless of one's awareness concerning the risks involved in an activity, fears affect body and mind; they may be long-standing or based on events of the present moment.

- *Insecurities.* Self-doubt is problematic when widespread across PSC; anxiety becomes generalized and leads to uncertainty and pervasive stress.

- *Inhibitions.* Self-imposed restraints and restrictions, particularly in the social domain, serve the purpose of keeping oneself out of trouble. Although inhibitions and self-control appear similar because they both result in a lack of action, the motivations behind them are quite different. While restraint displayed in self-control may come from a deliberate and carefully thought out process, the inhibited person exhibits hesitancy, indecision, and obstruction.

### Subtypes of Fears, Insecurities, and Inhibitions

Sometimes a person may appear to be without fears, insecurities, and inhibitions because one acts with little hesitation and seemingly no concern for safety or potential negative consequences. But this display of bravado, boldness, and swagger may contradict the way a person feels towards a PSC; FII may still lurk behind the person's actions and result in the development of the following contrary qualities:

- *Sensation-seeking.* One makes choices based on an overpowering desire to experience stimulation at any cost to avoid a monotonous and banal lifestyle.

- *Extreme risk-taking.* A person may show impulsive reactions that reveal self-destructive tendencies, ready to fight without provocation and engage in impetuous, reckless pursuits involving highly dangerous activities. Conscious or unconscious motivations behind these behaviors may reflect the following internal conflicts:

> *A negative self-image, including PI, II, CI, and TI, consisting of dysfunctional and harmful identifications.*

> *A lack of insight into one's motivations.*

> *An unbalanced value system.*

> *A lack of self-discipline or self-restraint.*

> *A limited ability to think through problems and consider alternative actions.*

Risk-taking, however, is not always a reckless, impulsive response to PSC; it can be a bold, brave, and deliberate action, overcoming fears and hesitations for a noble cause. Qualities of this kind of risk-taking behavior may include:

> *Flexibility.* The ability to change and act quickly.

> *Resolute.* A willingness to confront an issue head-on, with intensity and endurance rather than a brief, careless, and foolhardy reaction.

> *Curiosity.* An interest in something new and innovative that requires one to take risks.

## Developing Fears, Insecurities, and Inhibitions

Personal history reveals factors that contribute to the development of fears, insecurities, and inhibitions. Although FII usually begin in one's early years, they often continue to influence a person throughout life. Feeling intimidated and developing an inferiority complex are bound together; they cause and reinforce FII in ways that include:

- *Intimidation.* A confrontation with someone or something deemed powerful and forbidding may cause one to surrender one's beliefs and principles. The person may lack the courage or the knowledge to fight back. One's personal background contributes to these feelings of intimidation as follows:

  > *The family setting.* Overly strict, judgmental, or punishing parents can have an immediate and continual impact on a person. When consistently humiliated by parents or siblings, depreciation and disparagement can become an integral part of the personality.

  > *The growing up years.* The limitations of a sheltered life can also contribute to social inhibitions and fearfulness. A child that grows up in a seemingly normal family and community may still be at risk for developing FII. When exposed to "only the best" and "never the worst" and thus protected from life's hardships, the child may not be prepared for the challenges of adulthood that lie ahead.

  > *The adult years.* FII can be a response to CTMI that occur as one moves from early adulthood through middle age and into the later years. Even with a stable childhood, crises and setbacks can cause strong FII to form at any point in one's life.

- *Inferiority Complex.* A core pattern of negative self-images flows throughout the *personality constructs (PCs)* when a person has feelings of inadequacy that begin in childhood. This sense of inferiority can result in the development of a negative *PI*, with *pathos* expanding over the entire personality. *II* and *CI* may also be affected by feelings of inferiority because one is more likely to make poor decisions in relationships and group involvements. *TI* may advance in a bizarre and destructive way. An inferiority complex can cause one to approach PSC in the following maladaptive ways:

> ➤ *Social withdrawal.* A person pulls away from problematic PSC, even when one urgently needs to face the issues.

> ➤ *Inner turmoil.* Although a person may not exhibit behavioral manifestations of FII, strong feelings of inadequacy are present. Hesitation or complete lack of action reveals the depth of one's feelings.

> ➤ *Aggressive response.* Rather than being intimidated, a person's reactions to PSC may be hostile and antagonistic.

The need to avoid certain PSC is often so strong that one's response to FII becomes resistant to change. As a person continues to dodge PSC that cause FII, his TFA may no longer be deliberate but become unconscious automations. This ingrained pattern of response can result in the following:

- *Anticipatory anxiety.* Expecting and envisioning the feared PSC, one's imagination causes an overreaction, compounding FII in the process.

- *Expansion of FII.* When one does not take action to respond to the PSC appropriately or even attempt to reduce these feelings by reflecting on them, they will become self-perpetuating.

- *Contagious.* Fear can quickly spread to others with whom the person interacts.

## Issues in Fears, Insecurities, and Inhibitions

FII do not exist in a vacuum; when they continue unabated and dominate a person's TFA, long-term adverse effects on the entire personality may occur, including:

- *Lack of clarity.* Continual distractions, possibly combined with the blockage of cognitive-emotional connections and the censoring and editing of TFA. FII impacts cognitive functioning by compromising problem-solving abilities with:

> *Indecisiveness.*

> *Clouding over of thoughts.*

> *Confused, disjointed reasoning.*

> *Inability to complete tasks.*

> *Simplistic strategizing.*

> *Poor integration of materials.*

> *Hesitation in taking reasonable risks.*

- *Lack of energy.* A continual drain of a person's resolve, strength, and stamina. FII can consume the body and mind to the point of exhaustion.

- *Emotionalism.* Destructive reactions including disabling anxiety, panic, anger, overwhelming worry, and unrelenting feelings of guilt.

- *Lack of confidence.* Self-doubt that causes one to question every move.

- *Demoralization.* Discouragement—often associated with depression, anger, or anxiety—resulting in poor follow-through. *Directives* become directionless.

- *Self-deception.* The censoring and editing of TFA.

- *Lack of trust.* Suspicious and mistrusting of another person's motivations and actions.

- *Poor decision-making. PI, II, CI,* and *TI* that are not in sync but confused, unbalanced, and even contradictory. The dominance of emotional reactions to PSC interferes with the ability to think through an issue's complexities.

Ways to overcome FII include:

- *Examine what lies behind FII.*

  > *Is PI fragile and uncertain?* What personal identifications represent strength and fortitude?

  > *Are personal relationships and group affiliations unstable and erratic, further deepening FII?* Are connections available that offer more consistency and reliability that can enhance one's resolve to overcome FII?

  > *Is there a sense that past trauma or other stressful experiences may be behind the development of FII?* Is there a way to become more aware of these influences to help reduce their impact?

  > *Are directives imbalanced, further exacerbating FII?* Can values be sorted out to support a sense of calm and confidence?

- *Approach FII directly:*

  > *Confrontation.* To regain control, one must challenge FII, as they will not simply go away.

  > *Continuance.* Recognize and understand the elements that reinforce FII.

  > *Courage.* Make a vigorous and determined effort to overcome FII.

  > *Confidence.* Create a precise action plan to face FII. Practice may not make perfect, but it can help the person gain confidence in expressing oneself. In particular, role-playing can help a person develop strategies for responding to problematic PSC.

  > *Consistency.* Communication and assertiveness will only be effective when compatible with *PI, II, CI, TI, pathos,*

*directives*, and *spiritus*. A person must choose approaches aligned with one's emotional and intellectual style. For
example, a methodical person needs to develop strategies
consistent with an orderly approach to PSC.

# CHAPTER XXI QUESTIONS

1. What do you fear?

2. What kinds of PSC make you feel vulnerable and uncertain?

3. What PSC currently causes you to be hesitant or indecisive?

4. How do you handle PSC that are intimidating?

5. Do you take unnecessary risks?

6. Do you have self-doubts that interfere with your TFA?

7. How have they affected your ability to function?

8. Where do you think these hesitations and anxieties originate?

9. What steps do you take to overcome these anxious and uneasy feelings?

# XXII.
# ADVERSE CYCLICAL RECURRENCES

The hero of the 1993 movie *Groundhog Day* is Phil, a news reporter who becomes entrapped in space and time as he continues to re-experience the same day, repeating the same mistakes with the same outcomes. As he awakens each morning at 6:00 am, it is the day before, and the same events replay. At the movie's end, Phil finally learns from his mistakes and breaks free from a cycle of making poor decisions with unfortunate consequences, creating a brighter future for himself and the others in his life.

This idea that growth and forward movement occur when one is open to learning from experience is not new. A little more than a century ago, in his classic work *The Life of Reason* (1905-06), philosopher George Santayana wrote, "Those who cannot remember the past are condemned to repeat it." In the wake of World War II, statesman Winston Churchill echoed the wisdom of these words in a speech to the House of Commons, warning, "Those who fail to learn from history are doomed to repeat it." Warfare is the obvious example of the high cost of not learning from past errors in judgment. These failures, however, also play themselves out in everyday life as people continue to repeat behaviors that have detrimental consequences. Yet since the dawn of time, humanity has suffered this fate, the cycle of repeating one's mistakes and suffering its aftermath—*adverse cyclical recurrences (ACR)*.

## Defining Adverse Cyclical Recurrences

"To err is human…," but continuing to make the same mistakes that result in negative consequences goes beyond the limits of simple miscalculations and missteps; one is engaging in *ACR*. These errors in understanding, judgment, and decision-making occur for the following reasons:

- *Malicious intent.* Sometimes a person deliberately chooses to repeat actions that give the appearance of a mistake. These *ACR* are spiteful and often motivated by revenge, deliberate and calculated acts of sabotage.

- *A lack of planning.* Preparation is insufficient as a person continues to make the same blunders, gaffes, and oversights. One is not thinking ahead and seems blindsided when confronted with a problem even slightly out of the ordinary.

- *Improvisation stymied.* When a person rigidly holds onto inefficient approaches, the free flow of thoughts suffers, including imagination and creativity.

- *Carelessness.* Taking a casual and lackadaisical approach with a lack of self-discipline results in poor organization and follow-through.

- *Automations.* A person unknowingly continues the same behavioral patterns without focusing on the particulars of PSC or making adjustments.

- *Psychological dysfunction.* CTMI and emotionalism dominate the person's TFA, resulting in diminished reasoning.

- *Imbalance in directives.* When obsessions, compulsions, and addictions become the central focus, one does not reflect on the broader range of possible values.

**Subtypes and the Developing of Adverse Cyclical Recurrences**

Each of the elements of personality—*PI, II, CI, TI, pathos, directives,* and *spiritus*—increases the likelihood of the development of *ACR* when the following issues are present:

- *PI's qualities of practicality and objectivity are low.*

- *II and CI lack flexibility and insight in interpersonal or group involvements.*

- *TI follows a radical belief, and objectivity is lost.*

- *With pathos operating unconsciously, a person will be unaware of making necessary adjustments, even when a problem encountered seems straightforward, ordinary, and familiar, because of the following factors:*

    > *Emotional stress, indecisiveness, and vulnerabilities in conflicts.*

    > *Inflexibility in TFA due to the impact of traumatic events.*

    > *Diminished ability to consider the complexities and intricacies of PSC because of malevolent identifications.*

    > *Overreactions in emotionalism override reasoning, impacting ACR with:*

        o *Reactive and exaggerated responses.* Decisions tend to be erratic, unpredictable, confused, and contradictory.

        o *Low frustration tolerance.* Impatience results in poorly thought-through decisions.

        o *Inhibitions.* Hesitation in TFA leaves the person unable to initiate a response.

- *Imbalanced directives cause rigidity in TFA.*

- *Lack of awareness of spiritus's tendencies, including those that negatively affect TFA, reduces the ability to see the need to make adjustments.*

The likelihood of *ACR* increases with one or more cognitive deficiencies. They may occur throughout the spectrum of intellectual functions, including mental drive, focus, memory, logic, organizational thought, attention to detail, simplification, intuition, holism, perception, multidimensional thought, and inspired and original thought, causing impairments in the following areas of cognition:

- *Ability to listen and attend.*

- *Deductive reasoning.*

- *Preparation and arrangement of materials.*

- *Interpretation of data.*

- *Recognizing information overload.*

- *Trusting in one's instincts and understanding of PSC.*

- *Understanding the significance and underlying implications of PSC.*

- *Considering multiple factors simultaneously.*

- *Openness to new ideas.*

**Issues in Adverse Cyclical Recurrences**

Mistakes are part of the human condition, and while negative consequences occur, they also offer opportunities to learn from one's weaknesses and miscalculations. Learning from these encounters with PSC helps develop an understanding of oneself and those with whom one interacts. A person can enhance the ability to learn from mistakes and reduce the frequency and severity of *ACR* by addressing the following questions:

- *Cognitive discipline.* Does one's approach include organizational preparation?

- *Cognitive style.* Is one's approach too detailed or too abstract?

- *Decision making.* Are logic and deductive reasoning used exclusively, or do first impressions and gut instincts also play a role?

- *Communications.* How quickly are views and opinions stated? One can be too patient or not patient enough when interacting, with continued missteps in interpersonal relationships.

- *Perspective.* Is one aware of potential pitfalls and contradictions in approach?

- *Creative thinking.* Can one think "outside the box," or will one continue to use the same strategies regardless of PSC?

- *Energy.* Is one passive and retiring, displaying a lack of interests and involvements?

- *Past, Present, and Future.* Does a person consider the past, present, and future in attempting to understand PSC? They impact *ACR* in the following ways:

  > *The past.* Is awareness of the past important? The answer is yes; taking an intellectual and emotional perspective of bygone days is essential. But, if revisiting what has come before is simply a rehashing of old news, a type of self-flagellation, it will not be helpful. Negative emotions, including humiliation, depression, anger, anxiety, shame, or guilt, could be inadvertently reinforced by continually looking back, replaying old messages, and reliving painful emotions. But awareness of one's history can also allow a person to gain insights into one's TFA. Understanding the past can alert a person to the roles of emotional and intellectual vulnerabilities in problem-solving and decision-making approaches.

  > *The present.* Focusing on daily life is essential. A person

needs to be aware of the social dynamics of the moment, i.e., the invisible linkage between and among people. Attuned to TFA, one can make necessary distinctions and respond appropriately to each new PSC rather than using an overly generalized approach.

➤ *The future.* Planning and preparing offer a way to transverse the potential problems ahead. Thinking forward and developing alternate plans of action can help one overcome the unpredictability and uncertainty of what may be coming.

# CHAPTER XXII QUESTIONS

1. Do you sometimes make the same mistakes over and over?

2. What aspects of your personality keep this happening?

3. Do you have a general approach to problem-solving that works for you?

4. Do you attempt to alter your methods when you make the same mistakes?

5. Do you think about how you have handled PSC in the past?

6. Are you satisfied with how things are presently going?

7. Do you consider how best to handle PSC in future encounters based on past experience?

8. Can you bring people together to overcome problems?

9. Do you plan ahead to prepare for possible problems?

# XXIII.
# MATURITY: TO COME OF AGE

On January 15, 2009, a miracle occurred on the Hudson River. When Airbus A320 lost all engine power, Captain Chesley "Sully" Sullenberger safely glided the plane into the Hudson River, saving all 155 people aboard. Landing the craft in the freezing waters near Midtown, Manhattan, took more than the captain's extraordinary aviation skills and 30 years of experience, including serving as a USAF fighter pilot and certification as a glider pilot. Sully's focused, steadfast approach to the crisis was the difference between life and death. This ability to stay calm and adjust TFA at critical moments is the hallmark of maturity.

## Defining Maturity

It is not easy to transverse life's difficulties, including the give-and-take adjustments one must make in everyday encounters with PSC. Maturity is finding ways to maneuver through the developmental stages, with imagination and perhaps inspiration, in facing those challenges. Although it has features of conformity, maturity goes far beyond simply fitting into societal norms. It is the development of an independent spirit; being responsible and honoring one's commitments are its hallmarks. Coming of age includes integrating personality elements, fostering personal growth and empathetic concern for others, engaging in spiritual awareness, working out CTMI and emotionalism, balancing the value system, and understanding one's fundamental nature. Maturity may reveal itself through the elements of personality in the following ways:

- *PI.* Having well-attuned survival instincts with a keen sense of what is happening in one's world. A person is determined to develop individual qualities and attributes, and is tenacious in cultivating a unique personality, including:

> ➤ *Respect for oneself and others.*

> ➤ *A clear understanding of who one is and what one stands for.*

> ➤ *Endeavors to improve oneself while also having a concern for society's advancement.*

- *II.* Having a connection with others through empathy and straightforward communication.

- *CI.* Associating with groups that demonstrate both consideration for others while fostering personal development.

- *TI.* Engaging in a spiritual journey with a connection to a reality beyond the physical plane of existence.

- *Pathos.* Resolving CTMI and emotionalism. Thoughts, feelings, and actions (TFA) reflect reasonable standards.

- *Directives.* Balancing values with stable and consistent TFA. Obsessions, compulsions, and addictions are not controlling one's life and have not taken root in the fabric of the personality. Qualities of a value system that reflect maturity include:

> ➤ *Enjoying life while recognizing others' rights to the same.*

> ➤ *Conduct that is consistent and humane.*

> ➤ *Word and deed are bound together.*

> ➤ *Awareness of who one is, with minimal blocking of cognitive-emotional connections and censoring and editing TFA.*

- *Spiritus.* Awareness of one's essence, including inherent tendencies and qualities.

**Subtypes and Development of Maturity**

*Outliers,* the stand-alone *PCs* described in Chapter XX, Personality Constructs, impede the maturation process when they take center stage in one's life. The natural progression to the next developmental stage will then slow or stop, causing fixations and later regressions, which are related but to be distinguished, as follows:

- *Fixations.* An emotional impasse caused by unresolved critical issues in a developmental period. Becoming overly dependent on one or both parents is an example. Specific periods in a person's life offer the best opportunities for emotional growth; when this does not happen, fixations may occur. This lack of development creates vulnerabilities in the personality, with fixations offering a false sense of consistency and connectedness. The person "never grows up" and, as a result, seeks out dependent relationships upon entering adulthood. Fixations, principally the byproduct of *pathos,* continue to exist in the subconscious mind along with a multitude of other life experiences. They are *outlier PCs* from prior developmental periods, mainly formed out of unresolved CTMI.

  The concept that human development occurs one step at a time does not always apply; it depends on the overall functioning of the personality and the depth of the fixation. When some people experience fixations, they remain at that functioning level, whereas others move on to the next developmental period. Since each period has unique challenges, unresolved issues in one timeframe do not necessarily prevent a person from progressing to the next. A person's response to a particular developmental stage is largely independent of reactions to other periods, even though some influence will invariably be present. However, fixations will create vulnerabilities, and it is likely that under stress, a person will "go back" (regress) to those earlier stages. Revisiting the emotional level of development from a previous time, a 50-year-old person becomes a 10-year-old who throws a temper tantrum.

Beginning in childhood and continuing through adulthood, a person may experience a series of traumatic or highly stressful events that result in one or more fixations. Through classical (associational) conditioning, trauma elicits emotional responses that may include fear, anxiety, anger, or sadness. When exposed to traumatic or other highly stressful events, a person may not completely recognize and understand its psychologically harmful nature. Experiences of abuse, for example, are often blocked, censored, or edited, with the person not fully aware of its continual effect. However, when exposed to similar PSC that were present in the original event, the fixation becomes evident. Other than traumatic or other highly stressful experiences, two other factors that cause fixations to occur include:

> *The result of incidental experiences, without a traumatic event.* A person may come from a smother-love background that results in a dependency-laden relationship with one or both parents. Similar emotional connections and associations can occur with a wide variety of PSC throughout a person's life. One settles into a protective environment, cocooned in safe, comforting, and reassuring involvements. Even though the person may not have experienced a traumatic or other highly stressful event, fixations can easily form under these conditions and result in a lifelong series of dependent relationships.

> *The products of unresolved CTMI.* Family dysfunctions, including inappropriate discipline, poor communications, and inconsistent emotional support, can cause fixations, usually involving dependency. These influences are not limited to one's childhood years; they may occur at any time in a person's life.

• *Regressions.* A process in which a person is psychologically functioning at one level of development and backslides to an earlier stage, thereby temporarily reducing emotional discomfort. Although they may occur in many ways, the most common forms come from:

▸ *Previous trauma or other highly stressful events.* Present-day PSC stressors cause the person to return to a previous fixation, a developmental period with unresolved issues. A PSC triggers an overreaction—fear, panic, rage, or any other strong emotion—because, emotionally, the person has subconsciously returned to that earlier time. Unpleasant encounters may result in a person continually "going back" to that event, wrapped in emotions with no exit. A vicious circle forms; the traumatic or highly stressful experience is mentally reoccurring, creating an emotional response that repeats the experience.

▸ *Present-day stress.* A person experiences pressures in life, triggering an emotional reaction that causes one to find refuge in an earlier developmental period unrelated to previous trauma or other highly stressful events. These are simply the difficulties of living, with uncertainty and confusion persisting as one tries to get through the day. A person may then retreat to a more peaceful and protected place because the unconscious seeks a "pressure-free" zone. This flight to an inner sanctuary is not a regression to an earlier fixation or other highly stressful past events. In these retreats, any similarities between current PSC involvements and previously encountered PSC are coincidental and unrelated to fixation-regression linkage.

**Issues in Maturity**

Once established, fixations and regressions tend to be resistant to change; they will interfere with the maturation process unless a person develops strategies to overcome them, including:

- *Breaking the cycle.* Involvements in other pursuits and discouraging rumination on the traumatic or highly stressful event.

- *Recognizing pain.* A heartfelt and honest acknowledgment of the emotional distress and discomfort.

- *Gaining perspective.* Painful experiences are significant but only one part of one's life. The person needs to put the traumatic or other highly stressful events alongside countless other aspects of life experiences.

- *Transforming the event.* As one becomes stronger and smarter, a transformation of the traumatic or other highly stressful event occurs. Like an alchemist who takes scrap metal and turns it into gold, one can reorder, rearrange, and reconfigure the TFA that dramatically affects one's identity.

# CHAPTER XXIII QUESTIONS

1. How have you made adjustments when faced with difficult PSC?

2. Do you usually accomplish what you set out to do?

3. Have you formed mutually beneficial relationships?

4. How do you balance your own needs and wants with those of others?

5. Do you carry grudges, or can you just let them go and move on?

6. Do you have regrets that weigh heavy on your mind?

7. Have you over-relied on others?

8. Do you have difficulty making decisions and following through with them?

9. Have you sometimes felt frozen, unable to move forward with your goals?

10. Has it been tough to stand up to an adversary?

11. How do you handle it when another tries to do too much for you?

12. Do you sometimes act as you did when you were much younger?

13. How do you get yourself going again when you're not moving forward in a satisfying and productive way?

# XXIV.
# ADAPTATION: TO IMPROVISE, CHANGE COURSE, & OVERCOME

1889, Dayton, Ohio. With little fanfare, Orville and Wilbur Wright started up a small printing business, followed by a repair and sales bicycle shop; they later manufactured their own bikes. A keen interest in the possibility of human flight began in childhood when their father gave them a toy helicopter. Years later, after observing the ability of large birds to change the shape of their wings for turning and maneuvering, they developed the "wing-warping theory"; air flowing over the curved surfaces of the bird's wings created lift. During the next four years, they studied the wind's impact on large kites, similar to glider planes. They then built a wind tunnel, using powerful fans to move air against a stationary aircraft, allowing them to design more effective wings and propellers. Kitty Hawk, North Carolina, became the next base of operations; flying gliders gave them experience as pilots and a deeper understanding of how a plane would perform in the air.

Unsuccessful experimentation with these glider planes gave rise to doubt and discouragement, leading Wilbur to say, "Not within a thousand years would man ever fly." But they were tenacious and relentless; additional flights garnered more data, leading to the reconstruction of their gliders, followed by as many as a thousand successful flights, and finally, the installation of an engine. After more meticulous research, adjustments, and refinements, on December 17th, 1903, Orville flew the power-driven, heavier-than-air Kitty Hawk Flyer, proving that human flight was possible. The first successful motor-operated plane became a reality. Overcoming serious plane crashes and the skepticism of the time, they were vindicated. In 1909, the kings of Great Britain, Spain, and Italy came to see Wilbur's aeronautical displays. Later that year, the cover of *Harper's*

241

*Weekly* featured the Flyer circling the Statue of Liberty, with more than one million New Yorkers witnessing the flight. The key to the Wright brothers' success was adaptation.

## Defining Adaptation

Adaptation is a lifelong process of overcoming internal and external obstacles in the quest to develop, expand, and prevail, testing one's grit and resolve. Adaptation is the key to *striving toward clearmind*. It is not about becoming invincible but instead standing one's ground. By appraising personal strengths and weaknesses through the consolidation of experiences with PSC, one develops keen insights into personality and intellect.

## Subtypes and the Developing of Adaptation

This process begins when the mind opens to change as one explores the structure of personality, the process of thought, and the rhythm of life. Grasping the many nuances is challenging, and change is hard; adjustments in TFA can be disorienting and upsetting when one no longer has the security of the familiar. Perseverance makes a difference under these conditions playing a critical role in one's endeavors. Changes take place at any point in one's life through various ways: reflection or mentoring, life experience or formal schooling, success or failure. Some people do not seriously consider the possibility of adaptations in TFA, not even slight modifications in the approach to PSC. Others are comfortable making transitions, even radical ones.

Ideally, adjustments and attunements are an ongoing process whereby a person can come to terms with who one is, what one stands for, and where one is bound. Since nothing stands still and everything is in a continual flow, a person has little choice but to explore possibilities and departures from one's usual approaches to

PSC. Over 2500 years ago, the Greek philosopher Heraclitus stated, "The only constant in life is change." In light of this timeless observation, what follows is a description of the necessary interplay between adaptation and the *striving toward clearmind*.

**Issues in Adaptation: The Structure of Personality**

- *The personal identity.* A person defines the sense of who one is and what one stands for across situations and circumstances, resolving contradictions and inconsistencies. One looks at patterns in TFA, noting current functioning levels and how they have changed over the years.

- *The interpersonal identity.* Diverse and seemingly incompatible relationships one has had throughout a lifetime can come together. A person's review of one-on-one relationships with original and present-day families, marriage partners, coworkers, affiliations, and passing and momentary interactions helps to understand their cumulative effect.

- *The collective identity.* A person attempts to discover a common thread across group connections and forges a unified group identification. Exploring the impact of these affiliations allows one to see their similarities and contradictions.

- *The transpersonal identity.* The impact of a person's experience with the Divine is potentially dependent on many factors, including religious affiliations, family teachings, ethnic background, reading of sacred books, mentoring from elders, and academic coursework. Additionally, otherworldly (mystical) experiences with seemingly no scientific explanation can profoundly affect the development of *TI*. A deeper understanding of God and spiritual forces beyond intellectual awareness can develop throughout one's life, with insights and experiences becoming a single transpersonal identification.

- *Pathos.* Conflicts, traumas, malevolent identifications, and emotionalism—primarily unconscious and often insidious— can potentially have a sweeping and comprehensive impact on the personality. With adaptation, they are recognized, understood, and channeled. No longer threatening the entirety of the personality, they may become an advantage, a source of understanding and empathy. An awareness of one's history and emotional roots offer perspective and wisdom to a person's life. Rage and bitterness, depression and hopelessness, fragility and fear, can give way to awareness of inner struggles and a nonjudgmental acceptance of oneself and others. Taming the destructive power of *pathos* occurs through the process of adaptation as follows:

  ➤ *Conflicts.* The changing nature of life brings incompatibilities, inconsistencies, and disagreements that require compromise and concessions. The real troublemakers are unconscious childhood bedevilments that impact intimacy, independence, and integrity. These deeply rooted conflicts demand a sharper focus for adjustment and accommodation in clearing a path forward. Adaptation occurs when a person reconciles TFA by confronting inner turmoil and external demands.

  ➤ *Traumas.* Grievous and violent attacks, as well as the common insults and hurts of everyday life, are part of *pathos's* picture. While coming to terms with traumatic or other highly stressful events requires one to be fully aware of what has occurred, continually replaying the events will only reinforce the emotional pain and anguish. Overcoming obsessive thoughts by reframing events may be critical to the healing process.

  ➤ *Malevolent identifications.* One must recognize the destructive identifications linked to another person, institution, or even an idea; their roots are often paradoxical and confusing. When a person acknowledges and understands these identifications, their impact lessens. One can then explore the characteristics that have been adopted and make adjustments in TFA.

> *Emotionalism.* On conscious, semiconscious, or unconscious levels, a person has highly inappropriate emotional reactions to PSC and needs to address the cost to oneself and others. Besides rage reactions, emotionalism also includes long-standing anxieties, panic reactions, severe depressive episodes, fearful states, and ongoing grief, sadness, and regret.

- *Directives.* A person develops a value system that includes rating and ranking one's wants and needs. When hopes and dreams mesh with one's needs and expectations, the value system becomes balanced. Behavioral patterns may be inconsistent with one's feelings on many issues. A concerted effort is required to understand one's values and put *directives* in balance. A person recognizes that individuality needs consistency and cohesiveness to avoid *pathos's* onslaught of conflicts, traumas, malevolent identifications, and emotionalism.

The process of adaptation requires one to examine the correlation between stated values and the beliefs by which one lives. When a person remains locked into particular values set at an early stage of development, one's ability to adapt is minimal. Although they may no longer accurately reflect current wants, needs, or actions, one continues to express allegiance to them. Perhaps they give the person cover; but the stated convictions and subsequent actions reveal a completely different set of beliefs. They are then values in name only, theoretical and abstract, with no practical utility or meaning. Recognizing that values are not static and passive, a person may make adjustments to centrally important beliefs based on changing conditions, passing years, painstaking contemplations, and serious reflections. Clarifying one's values—including understanding their instability, inconsistency, and contradictory origins—enhances adaptation.

- *Spiritus.* As the most fundamental expression of a person's individuality, *spiritus* pervades the entirety of the mind. While a person can directly influence the other elements of the personality, *spiritus* acts as a constant as one adapts to changing PSC. Adaptation to PSC is easier when one accepts *spiritus* and gains an understanding of it, though an element of mystery will always remain. Acknowledging its nature, a person can better adjust to life's challenges, compensating for weaknesses and profiting from strengths. With deliberate attempts to examine TFA and by looking at behaviors over the years, one will further understand and connect to *spiritus.*

### Issues in Adaptation: The Process of Thought

- *Intellect.* A person shows adaptation when recognizing abilities and limitations, not only on a theoretical level but in practical terms. These cognitions involve many functions, principally among them are mental drive, concentration, memory, logic, organization, intuition, multidimensional thinking, creativity, and holism. After assessing each intellectual function, a person can develop ways to support strengths and compensate for weaknesses, helping adapt to problematic PSC.

- *Cognitive-personality connections.* When personality and intellect work together, a person can more easily make modifications in dealing with PSC. As one works through disharmonies, thinking is calm and clear with adaptations to contradictory and demanding PSC. With emotional and cognitive functioning in sync, understanding PSC is easy, and decision-making is straightforward. Addressing vulnerabilities in one's personality and thought processes leads to stable, consistent, and productive TFA. A person does not ignore emotional undercurrents, or allow them to dominate actions.

- *Optimal thinking.* One's capacity to think quickly and multi-task, limiting automations and habitual thought patterns, helps a person adapt. In assessing intellectual shortcomings, skill sets may complement one another with the following pairings: focused attention with simplification, logic with organization, objectification with flexibility of thought, and vision with coherence.

- *Sharpness.* Adaptation occurs when a person quickly spots the significance of people, situations, and circumstances (PSC) and handles them. Sharpness requires one to understand others' motives and the subtleties of PSC. This particular form of intelligence springs to life in a person's early years, fostered by survival instincts; one goes beyond theoretical and academic explanations. One considers the drive behind a person's or institution's actions: plans, programs, and timetables, examining the incentives and the bias' of others' efforts. With a full view of the anticipated encounter, a person is better able to make adjustments.

- *Strategic philosophy.* While sharpness means being aware of a person's or institution's motivations, *strategic philosophy* involves developing a guide to handle the full range of difficulties. Consciously and unconsciously, one maps out ways to deal with PSC complexities and contradictions. But one's *strategic philosophy* will only be an efficient planning manual that helps manage complications across a wide range of problematic PSC when a person benefits from feedback.

## Issues in Adaptation: The Rhythm of Life

- *Personality constructs.* Adaptation requires a person to become aware of "discrete personality clusters," including their degree of disharmony and dissimilarity. Through the identification process and based on cathexes (intense emotional connections), elements of personality will continue to form distinct personality entities—*PCs*—that are mostly independent of *PCs* already established. Becoming aware of the array of one's *PCs* and the triggers—people, situations, and circumstances (PSC)—that can set them off is essential for adaptation to occur. The ability to recognize divergent *PCs* helps one understand and adapt to contradictory TFA, including impulsive and out-of-character behaviors. Outlier *PCs*, triggered by idiosyncratic PSC, may become troublesome and result in unpredictable and incompatible actions. *PCs* will continue to form without notice or effort in the ordinary course of events over one's lifetime. By recognizing the diversity and contrariness among the *personality constructs*—even the unusual and reactive *PCs*—one can achieve stability, consistency, and balance among them, along with an alignment of TFA. A person can then make adjustments to ensure that highly conflicting *PCs* do not dominate actions at crucial moments in the decision-making process.

- *The clouding of mind.* Miscalculations, misjudgements, and inappropriate actions reveal the degree to which a person is overwhelmed by PSC. Exploring the etiology of FII helps one realize what identifications led to the development of these reactions and can help prevent them from becoming chronic conditions. Resolving FII may enhance the quality of one's relationships and communications. Overcoming FII requires a person to face them, building confidence in one's ability to make adaptations in life. FII potentially have some redeeming qualities; they can serve as a necessary reality check, allowing a person to take a step back and reconsider options.

- *Adverse Cyclical Recurrences.* Although repeated errors are painful and sometimes embarrassing, they can offer valuable insights and feedback. A lack of judgment, experience, knowledge, and intelligence are some of the common causes of mistakes. Vulnerabilities in the personality also play a part in the ability to learn from continual inaccuracies and omissions. Avoiding these slips and blunders is not as simple as it might seem. It requires determining the factors that play dominant roles leading to miscalculations and misreadings and then adjusting one's approach and understanding of PSC.

- *Maturity.* Self-sufficiency, independent thought, and interpersonal skills represent the hallmarks of maturity and are indispensable when changing course in midstream and making crucial decisions in a timely fashion.

In conclusion, adaptation implies that a person can improvise, change course, and overcome—requiring not only insights and acute perception but also courage and character. Survival instincts and empathetic concerns blend together, allowing the person to make the necessary adjustments. The identity has come together, *pathos* is not out of control, *directives* are balanced, and the person's nature is understood.

# CHAPTER XXIV QUESTIONS

1. What are your strengths?

2. What are your areas of vulnerability?

3. Can you compensate for those areas that are problematic?

4. Do you hang in there when the going gets tough?

5. How do you respond to setbacks?

6. How do your relationships influence your achievements?

7. Do you have a good understanding of the role emotions play in your life?

8. Can you look at hardships, failings, and setbacks in a new light and see how far you have come and what you have learned?

9. Can you see how your connections to people and institutions have influenced your TFA?

10. Have you been able to understand and control over-reactions to inconveniences and frustrations?

11. Can you let go of wants and needs that no longer work for you?

12. Can you prioritize your efforts to work on what is most important?

13. Have you learned from your mistakes and discovered why they have occurred?

14. How do you feel about your life and what you have been able to accomplish?

# REFLECTIONS

Caves are subterranean worlds that are mysterious and intriguing, winding and uncertain, deep and dark. They are unique in their grandeur and immensity. Exploring caves is enticing, adventurous, and wondrous, but it can also be scary and intimidating. Missouri's historic Meramec Caverns—hideout to the Jesse James gang—exemplify these qualities. Wandering through these underground chambers can be unsettling. Although uncertain of one's footing, the person forges ahead.

*Striving toward clearmind* can be likened to traversing the underground passages of caves as one uncovers the vast expanse of the mind. It is an exploration that requires vigilance and determination but, in return, offers acute insights into oneself and others. Unlike the established, enduring, and timeless caverns, the mind is in a constant state of transition and, potentially, transformation. Adaptation takes place with a forging ahead, making adjustments and advancements in one's purview of the world and position in it. Kaleidoscoping through life's confrontations and uncertainties demands being bold and brave while reshaping and revamping the ability to see oneself, PSC, and the continually changing nature of the world and everything in it.

# REFERENCES

Baum, Frank. *The Wizard of Oz*. George M. Hill Company, 1900.

Capra, Frank. *It's a Wonderful Life*. Liberty Films Studio, 1946.

Churchill, Winston. *Speech delivered before The House of Commons*, 1948.

Darabont, Frank. *The Shawshank Redemption*. Castle Rock Entertainment, 1994.

Grimm, Jacob & Wilhelm. *Snow White and the Seven Dwarfs*. Self-published, 1812.

Hand, David. *Snow White and the Seven Dwarfs*. Walt Disney Production, 1937.

Heraclitus. *Private writing*, 6th century B.C.

Marx, Groucho. *Quip delivered on several occasions*, 1949.

Nietzsche, Fredrich. *Twilight of the Idols*. Written in 1888 & self-published, 1889.

Paracelsus. *Private writings*, 16th century.

Plato. *The Apology*. Written between 399 & 387 B.C. Covers Socrates' defense of himself before the Athenian Council in 399 B.C.

Ramis, Harold. *Groundhog Day*. Columbia Pictures, 1993.

Sandburg, Carl. *Chicago*. Poetry Magazine, 1914.

Santayana, George. *The Life of Reason*. Self-published, 1905-1906.

Spielberg, Steven, along with several others. *Columbo*. Universal Studios, 1971-2003.

Tesla, Nikola. *Conversations with his Uncle Josip*, 1865.

Wright, Wilbur. *Statements made after a failed flight test*, 1901.

# ABBREVIATIONS & ACRONYMS

| | |
|---|---|
| ACR | Adverse cyclical recurrences |
| ADD | Attention deficit disorder |
| ADHD | Attention deficit hyperactivity disorder |
| CI | Collective identity |
| CPC | Cognitive-personality connections |
| CTMI | Conflicts, traumas, and malevolent identifications |
| FII | Fears, insecurities, and inhibitions |
| II | Interpersonal identity |
| IQ | Intelligence quotient |
| OC | Obsessive-compulsive |
| OCA | Obsessions, compulsions, and addictions |
| OT | Optimal thinking |
| PC | Personal construct |
| PI | Personal identity |
| PSC | People, situations, and circumstances |
| PTSD | Post-traumatic stress disorder |
| SP | Strategic philosophy |
| TFA | Thoughts, feelings, and actions |
| TI | Transpersonal identity |

# GLOSSARY OF TERMS

This glossary is a compilation of terms whose meanings are specific to this book; some of these definitions may be inconsistent with words and phrases in a standard dictionary.

**ABANDONING BALANCE.** To develop extreme values associated with deep-seated compulsions, moral bankruptcy, self-destructiveness, excessive moralizing, and perfectionism. (pp. 139-141)

**ABSTRACTION.** Generalizations made when drawing materials together by examining diverse materials. The distilling of characteristics reduces data to a set of essential features; it guides a person in constructing hypotheses and theories. (p. 161)

**ACQUIRED NEEDS.** Repetitive behaviors reinforced by the momentary reduction of stress. Addictions are the most common form of acquired needs, including alcoholism and drug abuse, excessive eating rituals, nonstop gaming, out-of-control gambling, and sexual preoccupations. (pp. 14-15)

**ACTIVE LISTENING.** To focus on the details of the communication, avoiding internal and external distractions. (p. 185)

**ADAPTATION.** A lifetime process of overcoming internal and external obstacles in the quest to develop, expand, and prevail. It requires appraising personal strengths and weaknesses and recognizing the impact of PSC as one consolidates experiences. (pp. 61-62, 242, 247-248, & 249)

**ADDICTIONS.** Obsessions and compulsions that involve both repetitive thought and action; physical or psychological dependencies that present as cravings, needs, wants, and indulgences that may take over a person's life. ( pp. 125 & 145-146)

**ADJUSTMENTS AMONG PCs.** Connections between particular PCs and PSC may cause some PCs to change in importance relative to other PCs. (pp. 209-210)

**ADVERSE CYCLICAL RECURRENCES (ACR).** Continuing to commit the same errors in understanding, judgment, and decision-making that result in negative consequences and happen for multiple reasons: malicious intent, a lack of planning, improvisation stymied, carelessness, automations, psychological dysfunction, and imbalance in directives. (pp. 225-226 & 248-249)

**AESTHETICS.** Principles or values used to judge something as fitting or appropriate by considering flow, congruency, consonance, and compatibility, with fitness, form, and symmetry held in high regard. (pp. 129-130)

**AGGRESSION** (see **CENSORING OF TFA**). A form of censoring that involves bullying another person through physical or verbal intimidation, threatening actions, or hostile interactions. (pp. 132 & 219)

**AGGRESSIVE AND HYPER-COMPETITIVE.** Dominating and perhaps humiliating another, with hostile tendencies valued over productivity and achievement. (pp. 29 & 219)

**AMBIGUITY.** Expressing oneself in an unintelligible and non-transparent way. (p. 193)

**ANALYTIC APPROACH.** The straightforward use of logic in contrast to the conceptual approach that relies on a holistic template. (pp. 30, 166-167, & 190)

**ANALYTIC COMPREHENSION.** Reaching a conceptual understanding by blending deductive reasoning and anticipation. (p. 190)

**ANTIAUTHORITARIANISM** (see **REBELLION**). Identification with oppositional behavior, challenging the establishment simply because it is there. (pp. 114 & 134)

**ANTICIPATION.** To foresee possible problems and proactively take the necessary precautions to prevent them from happening. (p. 164)

**ANTICIPATORY ANXIETY.** Expecting and envisioning the PSC that is feared causing the person to overreact. (pp. 49 & 219)

**ANXIETY.** Diffuse and scattered apprehension. (pp. 115 & 193)

**APPREHENSION** (see **FEARS, INSECURITY, & INHIBITIONS**). Fear, anxiety, and panic occur across the spectrum of PSC. (p. 115)

**ASSERTIVE.** Displaying confidence and leadership in positions and interactions. (p. 28)

**ATTENTION-SEEKING.** Wanting to be noticed and preferably the center of attention. (p. 135)

**ATTENTION TO DETAIL.** Carefully spelling out concrete, undeniable information that is sufficient to support one's position but not so detailed that the deeper understanding is lost. (p. 163)

**ATTITUDE.** A preconceived mindset that affects the emotional response. (pp. 36-37, 178, & 184)

**ATTUNED TO TACTICS AND CONTROLLING MANEUVERS.** Being aware of strategies used to persuade oneself and others. (p. 185)

**AUTHENTICITY.** Being true to oneself, aware of who one is and what one stands for, and the courage to take appropriate action. (pp. 82 & 121)

**AUTOMATIONS.** TFA repeated so often that they become mechanical, almost robotic, and no longer deliberate, resulting in a series of conditioned responses occurring without complete awareness. (pp. 60, 69-70, 177-179, & 226)

**AVOIDANCE** (see **CENSORING OF TFA**). Similar to suppression, a form of censoring in which the person thinks through a potentially negative interaction involving a PSC, weighing the pros and cons, and deciding not to get involved. (p. 132)

**AWARENESS** (see **CONSCIOUS STATES**; see **SEMICONSCIOUS STATES**; see **UNCONSCIOUS STATES**). Conscious, semiconscious, and unconscious TFA, shifting quickly and transforming from one to another and back again. Consciousness and awareness are interchangeable terms that describe a person's recognition and understanding of PSC. It does not break down into distinct states but occurs in gradations and approximations. (pp. 57-59, 70, 82, 123-124, 172, & 209)

**BALANCE.** A degree of steadiness, consistency, stability, and composure in the value system occurring on both conscious and unconscious levels. (pp. 28, 70, 121-122, 137-143, 191-194, & 227)

**BEING PRESENT.** Directing thoughts on what is currently happening, minimizing internal and external noise. (pp. 73 & 81)

**BELONGING.** Attraction to a group offering social status, stimulation, or a sense of inclusion and affinity. (p. 111)

**BIAS.** Repetitively experienced emotions that can affect a person's thoughts and actions. (pp. 27, 31, 36-37, 172, & 185)

**BLIND EYE EFFECT.** Commitment to a particular belief system and a reluctance to give it up, with objectivity lost or compromised. (pp. 200-201, & 226)

**BLIND SPOTS.** An almost complete lack of insight into oneself and PSC due to blocking, censoring, and editing effects. (pp. 141, 170, & 226)

**BLOCKING OF COGNITIVE-EMOTIONAL CONNECTIONS** (see **UNCONSCIOUS, TYPE 1**). An unconscious process that protects a person from fully experiencing the degree of pain radiating from pathos. Its immediate impact is that one does not face insecurities, imperfections, torments, traumas, and conflict, with a secondary effect in preventing a clear and complete view of reality. (pp. 40, 54, 60-61, 130-131, & 170)

**BODY LANGUAGE.** Whether overly communicated or covertly conveyed, physical movements that are part of PI and reflect a person's feelings and affect how others receive a message. (p. 80)

**BREAKING THE CYCLE.** Becoming involved in activities to help a person overcome entrapment in fixations, regressions, and ruminations associated with a traumatic event. (p. 238)

**BULLY-BOY TACTICS.** Forcefully making oneself known that then pressures others to conform. (p. 185)

**BUREAUCRATIC ZEAL.** Being caught up with rhetoric and ideas which take on a life of their own. (p. 111)

**CALMNESS.** Setting aside internal and external distractions. (p. 172)

**CAPACITIES.** Cognitive abilities based on habitual actions or carefully planned out acquired skills. (pp. 172-174)

**CARELESSNESS.** A lack of seriousness resulting in a neglectful, unstudied, and inattentive approach to relationships and activities. (pp. 112 & 226)

**CATHARSIS.** The expression of emotions toward a person, institution, possession, or idea, often experienced when a person's feelings are directly, loudly, and forcefully discharged. (p. 47)

**CATHEXIS.** The emotional energies that allow a connection to take place. It can be any emotion—love, infatuation, joy, enthusiasm, excitement, fear, disgust, affection, loathing, anger, hate, or anxiety. The more potent the emotion, the stronger the cathexis. (pp. 27-28, 45, 48, & 248)

**CAUTION TO NOT MISINTERPRET COMMUNICATIONS.** Taking care to realize that misleading or confusing messages and announcements may not be the product of a deliberate attempt to deceive. (pp. 185-186)

**CENSORING OF TFA.** A person's active suppression of a thought, feeling, or action, including avoidance, aggression, excessive cautiousness, and withdrawal, whereby one does not sufficiently consider or reveal what may be objectionable. (pp. 131-132)

**CENSORING AND EDITING OF TFA.** Although they may not be overtly displayed, the deliberate intent to commit a falsehood to make it difficult for others to follow one's line of thinking. It occurs principally when a person concludes there are adverse consequences to specific TFA. (pp. 131-133 & 170-171)

**CENTRAL PC.** Authority over other PCs, developing when an intense identification with someone or something occurs. (p. 209)

**CHARACTER ASSASSINATION.** A tactic used by persuade others by which a person repeatedly accuses someone of something malicious and harmful. (p. 185)

**CHARM AND ALLURE** (see **STYLE**). Attracted to the Hollywood look of things. (p. 111)

**CHEMISTRY**. The way in which people get along, affecting the development of II. (pp. 89-90)

**CIRCUMSTANCES**. Unexpected, unplanned, abrupt, and unforeseen events occurring when a person is already in a given situation. (p. 26)

**CLARITY**. Being understandable and well formulated. (pp. 122-124 & 219-220)

**CLARITY OF PCs.** PCs that form under confusing and stressful conditions are usually poorly developed, fragmented, and lacking transparency. (p. 210)

**CLASSICAL CONDITIONING** (see **UNCONSCIOUS, TYPE 4**). The process by which associations form through the intentional or accidental pairing of TFA. Automatic and without thought, these connections can become firmly entrenched and resistant to change, with no symbolic-psychological-emotional undercurrent involved in the process. (pp. 62-63 & 235)

**CLEARMIND**. A way to disentangle the psyche, freeing it from all that binds, unleashing the vast potential within every human being, expressed through an individual endeavor. (p. 3)

**CLOUDING OF MIND** (see **UNCONSCIOUS, TYPE 2**). Fears, insecurities, and inhibitions brought on by PSC that emotionally overwhelm a person. (pp. 215-222 & 248)

**CLUTTERED THOUGHTS**. Focusing, synthesizing, and drawing

conclusions become difficult, with ideas jumbled together if not altogether confused. (p. 144)

**CODEPENDENCY.** A shared overreliance on another encouraged by one or both parties. (p. 113)

**COGNITION** (see **INTELLECT**). A composite of interconnecting and interacting intellectual operations, akin to a computer processing mounds of data and drawing conclusions. (pp. 29-30 & 159)

**COGNITIVE-EMOTIONAL CONNECTIONS** (see **AWARENESS**; see **THE BLOCKING OF COGNITIVE-EMOTIONAL CONNECTIONS**; see **UNCONSCIOUS, TYPE 2**). The psyche's attempt at integrating and synthesizing unresolved CTMI through intellectual awareness and emotional understandings. (pp. 41-42, 60-61, & 130-131)

**COGNITIVE-PERSONALITY CONNECTIONS (CPC).** The continual interactions between cognitive processes and personality elements. (pp. 246-247 & 269-271)

**COGNITIVE PROCESSES** (see **INTELLECT**). The intellectual hardware that requires knowledge, learning opportunities, a willingness to listen intently, and an openness to change. (pp. 172-175)

**COHERENCE.** Being connected, unified, and congruent in thought, word, and deed with messages that are understandable, consistent, and consonant with each other. (p. 162)

**COLLECTIVE IDENTITY (CI).** The qualities and characteristics that develop through a person's connections with groups. (pp. 5, 93-94, 153, 234, & 243)

**COMMAND AMONG PCs.** A central PC with authority over other PCs. (p. 209)

**COMMON SENSE.** Being aware of what is obvious, clear, and evident. (pp. 123 & 162)

**COMMUNICATIONS.** The "how" of the message conveyed (the manner and tone) and the "what" (the words spoken) determine its meaning and significance. (pp. 12, 89, 172-173, 185-186, & 229)

**COMPLEX** (see **INFERIORITY COMPLEX**; see **PRIMA DONNA COMPLEX**). A conscious or unconscious pattern of thoughts, feelings, or actions (TFA) organized around a theme. (pp. 6, 107, 112, 135, & 218-219)

**COMPLEXITIES.** When the nature of PSC is challenging to understand because it is sophisticated and involved, often occurring because the content is inherently problematic and multifaceted. (p. 31)

**COMPLICATIONS.** When many variables do not seem to go together as expected, preventing connections from forming in a meaningful way. (p. 31)

**COMPULSIONS.** Repeated behaviors that are usually ritualistically performed to momentarily reduce anxiety or fear. (pp. 139 & 144-145)

**COMPULSIVITY** (see **EDITING OF TFA**). A form of editing that involving rigidly adhering to a set schedule and standard, missing nothing to avoid the possibility something could go wrong. (p. 133)

**CONCENTRATION** (see **FOCUS**).

**CONCEPTUAL APPROACH.** A holistic or big-picture understanding of PSC under study in which one develops insights by looking for the guiding principles that underlie PSC. (p. 30)

**CONCEPTUALIZATION.** A higher level of abstraction that involves mapping out specific elements and their relationships. (pp. 161 & 202)

**CONCEPTUALIZATION AFFECTED BY COGNITIVE-PERSONALITY CONNECTIONS.** One's understanding of the knowledge acquired—impacted by its significance for the person—leading to the forming of a concept. (pp. 172-174)

**CONDITIONING TO STIMULI.** The tendency to form associations with PSC quickly and strongly, leading to a repetition of the response to certain stimuli (pp. 62-64)

**CONFLICTS.** Disagreements within oneself or with others that create an internal struggle over issues involving aggression, assertiveness, intimacy, achievement, ambition, trust, or independence. (pp. 6, 109, & 243)

**CONFUSION.** When one's understanding of PSC lacks organization and makes no sense. (p. 31)

**CONNECTIONS AMONG PCs.** The similarity and intensity of one's experiences that affect the development of the PCs and the consistency of behaviors. (p. 210)

**CONNECTIONS: INTERPERSONAL RELATIONSHIPS.** Interactions that may or may not be meaningful, significant, or stimulating. (p. 133)

**CONSCIOUSNESS.** The degree to which awareness permeates the personality. (pp. 13, 21, 82-83, 120, 131, 194, & 198-199)

**CONSCIOUS STATES.** Thoughts that are deliberate, calculated, intentional, and purposeful; a full awareness of the images and ideas formed. (pp. 57-58, 120, & 198-199)

**CONSISTENCY.** Stated beliefs and actual behaviors are in harmony, with congruency in thoughts, words, and deeds. (pp. 122, 137, & 221-222)

**CONSONANCE.** When the elements of the personality are in harmony. (p. 84)

**CONTEXT.** To put one's history in perspective with reference points. (p. 81)

**CONTROLLING.** A restrictive and rigid approach to interpersonal relationships characterized by over-directing and over-managing others. (p. 116)

**CONVENTIONALISM.** A way of life that offers a sense of security, safety, and serenity, with a preference for domestic routines, interpersonal contacts, and regularities in one's comings and goings. (p. 125)

**DATA GATHERING APPROACH.** To collect as much information as possible, and then as if working on a puzzle, put the accumulated data in place to form a complete picture. This approach is empirical and dedicated to understanding the details of PSC. (p.30)

**DECISION-MAKING.** The ability to troubleshoot and understand the different parts of a problem. (p. 116, 220, & 229)

**DECISIVENESS.** Knowing when the time for pausing and reflecting is over and choosing a course of action has arrived. (pp. 174 & 220)

**DEMORALIZATION.** Discouragement often associated with depression, anger, or anxiety (p. 220)

**DEPENDENCY.** A passive role in relationships, over-relying on others to make decisions. (pp. 113 & 193)

**DIRE CONSEQUENCES.** Repercussions often used as threats if a person does not follow another's dictates. (p. 185)

**DIRECTIVES.** The guiding principles and values that each person adopts and lives by that are internal, intrinsic, and ingrained. (pp. 7, 119-124, 153, 170, 181-182, 199, 226, 234, & 245-246)

**DISAPPOINTMENT OVER ONE'S HANDLING OF PSC.** Distress caused by decisions made. (p. 39)

**DISILLUSIONMENT BASED ON A LOSS OF STATUS.** The result of the perception that one's standing, position, or role in life has diminished. (p. 39)

**DISORGANIZATION.** An unsystematic approach to PSC. (p. 193)

**DISPLACEMENT.** An indirect expression of TFA toward someone or something unrelated or tangentially related to the original provocation or cause. (p. 40)

**DISTRACTION.** Anything that limits or affects a person's train of thought and causes a loss of focus on the task at hand. (pp. 182-184 & 219-220)

**DIVERSE EXPERIENCES FORMING A COHERENT PI.** The integration of complex and challenging events in a person's life, especially difficult when they have been conflicting, incompatible, or inconsistent. (p. 83)

**DOMINATION.** An overwhelming need to control others. (pp. 113-114)

**DRAMATICS.** Histrionic, theatrical, and emotionally extreme behaviors, with a person striving to be noticed, accepted, and rewarded. (p. 193)

**DREAM STATES** (see **UNCONSCIOUS, TYPE 8**). A form of thought and communication, whether or not the messages are received or understood; narratives occur in words, images, and feelings. Dreams are the most vivid example of the unconscious mind expressing itself. A symbolic-psychological-emotional undercurrent may be present. (pp. 65-66 & 124)

**EDITING OF TFA.** The active altering, revising, correcting, changing, or expunging of a TFA in attempts to change its status or meaning and include rationalization, intellectualization, and compulsivity. (pp. 132-133)

**ELEMENTS OF PERSONALITY.** A person's individual qualities and characteristics, including identity, unresolved issues, values, and inherent traits. (p. 3)

**EMOTIONAL CHRONICITY.** The characterological quality of emotional responsivity that represent the depth of a person's attributes and traits. (p. 49)

**EMOTIONAL COMBINATIONS AND SHIFTINGS.** The blending and combining of feelings occurring simultaneously. (p. 48)

**EMOTIONAL CONNECTIONS.** Cohesion and kinship that may enhance a feeling of closeness. (p. 90)

**EMOTIONAL CONSEQUENCES.** The outcomes, sometimes devastating, that come from emotional reactions. (p. 49)

**EMOTIONAL DEPTHS.** The intensity and fluidity of particular emotional reactions, traits, states, flow, and remembrances that depend upon a person's natural inclinations and the PSC involved at the time. (p. 48)

**EMOTIONAL DISCHARGE** (see **CATHARSIS**). A cathartic release of distressing sensations and uncomfortable feelings that cannot substitute for a cognitive-emotional connection. (p. 47)

**EMOTIONAL EXPERIENCES.** The ways in which a person feels and takes in current everyday life events. (p. 70)

**EMOTIONAL EXPRESSION.** The ways in which a person reveals emotions, including reactions, traits, states, flow, and remembrances. (pp. 46-47)

**EMOTIONAL FLOW.** Inwardly felt or outwardly demonstrated, a merging of one's feelings with the thinking process that is reflective and deliberate. (pp. 46-47)

**EMOTIONAL INDIVIDUAL DIFFERENCES.** The varied ways people take in and express their feelings about inner and outer life experiences affected by biological predispositions, life experiences, and spiritus. (p. 48)

**EMOTIONAL INTERNAL RESPONSES.** Strong emotional reactions that occur simply from thinking about an event. (p. 49)

**EMOTIONALISM/EMOTIONALITY.** Extreme emotional responses creating a pattern of overreactions beyond what would be considered reasonable or appropriate. It is a chronic condition, including rage, deep depression, severe panic, debilitating anxiety, and paralyzing fear may dominate a person's life. (pp. 6-7, 50-51, 111-116, 131, 137-138, 201, 208, 220, & 245)

**EMOTIONAL MEMORIES** (see **EMOTIONAL REMEMBRANCES**). To vividly recall events in one's life and intensely reexperience the emotional component. (p. 21)

**EMOTIONAL PROPENSITY.** The predisposition to react emotionally to PSC. (p. 70)

**EMOTIONAL REACTIONS.** A sudden surge in feelings involving the element of surprise, a reflexive reply to a perceived change in a person's life, or perhaps a misperception or misinterpretation of events. (pp. 46, 59, & 171-172)

**EMOTIONAL REACTIONS' SUBTYPES.** Whether expressed or kept inside, they include emotionalism, feigned emotions, hysteria, hypersensitivity, insecurity, negativism, rebellion, inhibition, empathy, and passion. (pp. 50-53)

**EMOTIONAL REACTIVITY.** Partially predetermined by a predisposition, the degree to which one experiences and expresses feelings about PSC, including trends toward anger, anxiety, and depression. (pp. 69 & 171-172)

**EMOTIONAL REMEMBRANCES** (see **EMOTIONAL MEMORIES**). Past emotional experiences that flood back into the personality. (pp. 47 & 54)

**EMOTIONAL STABILITY.** On conscious and unconscious levels, emotionalism is not able to gain control of TFA. (pp. 11 & 192-193)

**EMOTIONAL STATES.** Transient feelings brought on by a person's physical condition. (p. 46)

**EMOTIONAL TRAITS.** Enduring and ingrained feelings in a person's character. (p. 46)

**EMOTIONAL VISCERAL QUALITY.** The physical quality of emotions that is revealing and often more powerful than spoken words, including a facial expression, a handshake, or tone of voice. (p. 49)

**EMOTIONS.** The feelings and responses central to a person impacted when the external world of PSC and the internal processing of those events collide. (pp. 45-54, 171, & 208)

**EMPATHETIC APPROACH.** When emotional identifications guide in decision-making with the person relying heavily on feelings. (p. 30)

**EMPATHY.** A feeling state in which a person forms an emotional connection to another's experience, a linkage that is visceral and emotional. (pp. 53, 108, 110, & 172)

**EMPTYING OF THE MIND.** Letting go of obsessive thoughts and, in particular, their emotional links. (p. 73)

**ENDURANCE.** When a person reacts to physical or emotional hurt with the forming of a lasting identification. (p. 22)

**ENERGY** (see **CATHEXIS**). The power of any emotion or group of emotions to fuel the connections between a person and PSC: love, warmth, coldness, acceptance, rejection, infatuation, joy, enthusiasm, excitement, fear, disgust, affection, loathing, anger, meanness, callousness, and anxiety. (pp. 28, 69-73, & 220)

**ENERGY LEVELS AND PERSONALITY.** The ways in which the effects of emotions drain or replenish the resources needed to navigate challenging PSC. (pp. 69-70)

**ENVIRONMENTAL PRESS.** The outer world of people, situations, and circumstances (PSC). (pp. 25-26, 83-84, & 122)

**EUREKA EXPERIENCES.** Spontaneously becoming aware of spiritual realities, and exploring the experiences to a fuller degree. (p. 103)

**EVERYDAY INCIDENTS (OF STRESS).** Emotional responses from life events that form associations, sometimes reexperienced when exposed to similar PSC. (p. 54)

**EXCESSIVE CAUTIOUSNESS** (see **CENSORING OF TFA**). A form of censoring that is a pause, a wobbling, or faltering that happens because of fear that involves being overly careful, hesitating, or procrastinating. (p. 132)

**EXAMINATION OF THE DATA**. A systematic, organized, and highly structured approach to grasp the underpinnings of PSC. (p. 190)

**EXPECTATIONS**. A strong belief that an event will have a particular outcome. (pp. 37 & 140-141)

**EXPERIENTIAL LEARNING** (see **UNCONSCIOUS, TYPE 6**). Comprehension even with minimal instruction or preparation due to involvement and participation in an activity. (pp. 64 & 83)

**EXPLOITATION**. People being equated to commodities with no intrinsic worth. (pp. 114 & 128)

**EXTRAORDINARY COMPENSATION**. Personal achievements helping to overcome self-doubts and uncertainty. (p. 112)

**EXTERNAL NOISE**. The daily stress from PSC, varying in its significance and the degree to which it depletes energy resources. (p. 72)

**EXTERNAL WORLD** (see **PEOPLE, SITUATIONS AND CIRCUMSTANCES/PSC**). A person's interactions with PSC and their impact on TFA. (p. 123)

**EXTRANEOUS FORCES IMPACT ON VALUES**. Concessions made due to political pressures, unrealistic deadlines, or other stressors caused by PSC. (pp. 142-143)

**EXTREME RISK-TAKING**. Impetuous and perhaps reckless pursuits involving highly dangerous activities, which may or may not be appropriate to the PSC. (pp. 216-217)

**EXTREMISM.** TFA that are self-destructive and significantly outside of standard actions and reactions. (p. 202)

**FAITHFULNESS.** Unquestioned belief and commitment to God, a continual presence that brings peace, serenity, and strength. (p. 129)

**FAMILY RELATIONSHIPS.** The child's one-on-one relationships with parents and siblings resulting in adopting their characteristics and developing II in the process. Families also have a collective impact on the child as well. (pp. 88 & 94)

**FANTASIZING.** Taking journeys of the imagination, which may bring fresh ideas or unrealistic beliefs and denial of realistic concerns. (pp. 179-180)

**FEARS.** Reactions to PSC that can affect both the body and the mind occurring when someone or something is upsetting. (pp. 115, 138, 215-216, & 244)

**FEARFULNESS.** Reacting to PSC with apprehension and alarm, even when no significant risk is involved. (p. 127)

**FEARS, INSECURITY, AND INHIBITIONS (FII)** (see **APPREHENSION**). Originating from stressors in the environment or forming entirely in the imagination, potentially allowing a person to remain vigilant of difficulties with PSC, but can be problematic when flowing out of conflicts, traumas, and malevolent identifications (CTMI). Operating on conscious, semiconscious, and unconscious levels of awareness can further compound and compromise a person's TFA. (pp. 115, 127, 215-222, & 248)

**FEEDING THE BIAS.** Reinforcing populist notions, leanings, and preferences, employing subtle or flagrant manipulation. (p. 185)

**FEELINGS OF FAILURE.** Repetitive self-blaming, even though the person may work in earnest. (p. 39)

**FEIGNED EMOTIONS.** Acting, a consciously thought-out performance to manipulate and fool another person with possible motives that include gaining sympathy, disrupting communication, or confusing and controlling PSC. (p. 51)

**FIRST THOUGHTS AND FIRST ACTIONS.** One initially has ideas, "first thoughts," about involvements with particular PSC that lead to an immediate response, "first actions." These "first thoughts" persist and may become ingrained, so when similar encounters with PSC occur, a linkage rapidly forms with the "first actions." (p. 179)

**FIXATIONS.** An emotional impasse caused by unresolved developmental issues, creating vulnerabilities in the personality. (pp. 235-236)

**FLASHBACKS** (see **POST TRAUMATIC STRESS DISORDER/ PTSD**). The re-experiencing of a traumatic event, reappearing when triggered by an image, thought, memory, or encounter. Suddenly, typically laced with fear, overwhelming anxiety, and panic, it is back in full force and can be debilitating, catastrophic, and emotionally exhausting. (p. 54)

**FLEXIBILITY.** Displaying a willingness to make adjustments in TFA. (pp. 137, 164, 192, & 217)

**FLOW STATE.** A person functioning at maximum capacity regardless of PSC's intrusive or disruptive qualities, occurring when optimal thinking is at its zenith. (pp. 182-184)

**FOCUS** (see **SUSTAINED ATTENTION**). To filter out distractions by subduing inner and outer noises of everyday life. Anything that limits or affects a person's train of thought can affect the ability to focus. (pp. 160 & 173)

**FORTHRIGHT AND AUTHENTIC** (see **AUTHENTICITY**). TFA expressed when a person resolves the negativity and emotionalism of pathos and overcomes blocking, censoring, and editing. (p. 82)

**FRUSTRATION TOLERANCE.** Patience results in decisions being thought through and efficiently performed. (p. 172)

**GAINING PERSPECTIVE.** Traumatic events put in the context of one's entire life alongside many other experiences. (p. 238)

**GENUINENESS** (see **AUTHENTICITY**). When TFA are in line with one another—integrated, consistent, and compatible. (p. 194)

**GNOTHI SEAUTON (KNOW THYSELF).** Words carved into stone at the entrance of the Temple of Apollo at Delphi in Greece. (pp. 120-121)

**GOOD OLE BOY NETWORK.** Those in positions of power make decisions, mostly affecting those unaware of the discussions. (p. 185)

**GRIEVING.** Unrelenting sad feelings due to loss, commonly of a person or a beloved pet. (pp. 39 & 111)

**GROUNDING.** A straightforward, concrete, and factual approach to problem-solving. (pp. 83 & 101-102)

**GULLIBILITY.** Not taking or holding positions, believing that all truths—if they represent anything at all—are malleable and open to interpretation. The person is vulnerable to half-baked "truths" and easily persuaded, not having adequately reflected on the relevant issues. (p. 201)

**GUILT.** Remorse over one's actions or lack thereof. (p. 39)

**HABIT PATTERNS** (see **UNCONSCIOUS, TYPE 4;** see **UNCONSCIOUS, TYPE 5**). A series of conditioned responses which can be the product of associations formed on either a conscious or unconscious level. (pp. 62-64 & 179-181)

**HARDENED.** A person learns to fend for oneself under trying conditions, developing resilience. (p. 191)

**HARMONY.** Stability, consistency, and congruency in one's beliefs and actions. (pp. 81 & 122-123)

**HOLISM.** An overarching view, understanding the long-term implications of problem areas and the decision-making process. (pp.165-166)

**HOSTILITY.** Aggression expressed physically, verbally, passively, or internally. (pp. 108 & 193)

**HUMANISM AND ALTRUISM.** Expressions of concern for others, acts of kindness, or involvement in organizations that help those in need. (p. 129)

**HYPERSENSITIVITY.** Being easily offended, with extreme emotional reactions; overwhelmed when exposed to the slightest hardships. (pp. 51-52)

**HYSTERIA.** Overreactions, over-dramatizations, or exaggerated actions and behaviors that are highly manipulative and theatrical, possibly seductive and provocative. (p. 51)

**IDENTIFICATION PROCESS.** When emotional connections, which may be complicated and enigmatic, strongly impact a person's view of oneself on conscious and unconscious levels. The identification process culminates with the blending together of personal identity (PI), interpersonal identity (II), collective identity (CI), and transpersonal identity (TI). An emotional component is always present, giving force, passion, energy, and endurance to the formation of the identity. (pp. 19 & 21-22)

**IMMATURE.** Not readily accepting responsibilities; not acting reasonably or reliably. (p. 29)

**IMPRACTICALITY.** An overly theoretical approach to PSC with an unrealistic problem-solving strategy. (pp. 116 & 194)

**IMPULSIVENESS.** Actions that are impulsive, hasty, and careless, without consistency or considering possible consequences. (p. 193)

**INACCURATE AND DISTORTED PERCEPTIONS.** No longer seeing things as they are, with minimal awareness, misrepresentation, exaggeration, or habitual lying. (pp. 120-121)

**INACCURATE CONCEPTUALIZATIONS.** Mistaken ideas about people, institutions, or society that lead to faulty understandings and unsound decisions. (p. 202)

**INAPPROPRIATE INTERACTIONS.** An overly sensitive attitude that becomes apparent when a person reacts strongly to criticism, disapproval, or rejection. (p. 113)

**INCIDENTAL EMOTIONAL GAIN.** An indirect, accidental, and unintentional response that results in a benefit. (p. 37)

**INCONSISTENCIES.** TFA conflict in irreconcilable ways. (p. 112)

**INDEPENDENCE.** To decisively and confidently take positions guided by principles and a set of ideas about how the world works. (p. 192)

**INFERIORITY COMPLEX.** A core pattern of negative self-images that flows throughout the personality constructs (PCs) and may result in developing a negative PI. (pp. 218-219)

**INFORMAL LEARNING.** Street smarts acquired through exposure to life's challenges, including developing an acute understanding of PSC. (p. 174)

**INFORMATION OVERLOAD.** When data overwhelms people and institutions with reports, bulletins, and news items that are confusing, contradictory, or irrelevant. (pp. 162-163)

**INHIBITIONS.** The suppression of TFA causing self-imposed restraints, restrictions, and mental blocks, driven by fears of failure, consequences, humiliation, or simply the unknown. (pp. 40, 52-53, & 216)

**INITIAL LISTENING.** The mind is fully engaged and "locks in" with minimal distraction when first exposed to a challenge. It is essential to understand the information from the beginning as one lays the groundwork for determining the next step. (p. 160)

**INNER AWARENESS.** PI expands with the development of perspective, stillness and presence, harmony, consciousness, authenticity, maturity, and moral reasoning. (p. 81)

**INNERMOST INTENT.** The thoughts, feelings, and principles that guide a person's actions. (p. 122)

**INNER STRENGTH.** Learning to persevere under challenging conditions, a person develops a deep resolve to fight on when all seems lost. (p. 110)

**INSECURITIES.** Problematic self-doubt that is diffuse and pervasive across PSC. (pp. 52, 114-115, & 216)

**INSPIRED AND ORIGINAL THOUGHT**. When imagination breathes life into an idea. (p. 165).

**INSTABILITY**. Displaying a lack of self-control with impulsiveness and reactiveness, possibly with fits of anger. (p. 112)

**INSTINCTS** (see **UNCONSCIOUS, TYPE 7**). Subliminal, visual, and visceral feelings that offer an impression about PSC on a level beyond logic or deductive reasoning. (pp. 15-16, 65, & 167)

**INSTINCTUAL APPROACH** (see **NATURAL INSTINCTS APPROACH**). Going with an intuitive hunch based on experiential knowledge and awareness. (p. 30)

**INSTRUMENTAL CONDITIONING** (see **UNCONSCIOUS, TYPE 5**). TFA are reinforced through rewarding or punishing of a person's responses. (pp. 63-64)

**INTEGRATION OF VALUES**. Wants and needs in sync with the entire personality. (p. 123)

**INTELLECT** (see **UNCONSCIOUS, TYPES 3 AND 6**). Cognitive functions that include mental drive, initial listening, sustained attention, memory, logical thought, objectification or realism, practical reasoning, coherence, organization, simplification, attention to detail, intuition, openness to experience, perception, multidimensional thinking, inspired and original thought, and vision. (pp. 159-167 & 246)

**INTELLECTUALIZATION** (see **EDITING OF TFA**). A form of editing that involves taking facts and bending them to be consistent with one's positions, with statements bearing enough resemblance to the truth that they will pass for the truth. (p. 133)

**INTELLECTUAL LAZINESS**. A lack of interest or energy in thinking through issues. (p. 201)

**INTELLECTUAL SELF-DISCIPLINE.** A commitment to learning, thinking, and problem-solving. (pp. 173-174)

**INTELLECTUAL UNDERSTANDINGS.** PI expands with the development of knowledge, perception, and synthesis of one's experiences. (p. 82)

**INTENTIONAL EMOTIONAL GAIN.** The direct and deliberate manipulation of PSC to take advantage of another to benefit oneself. (p. 38)

**INTERESTS.** Curiosity and attraction to objects or activities. (p. 142)

**INTERNALIZATION.** Blocking, editing, and censoring of TFA, possibly resulting in the partial and temporary dismissing of psychologically painful states. (p. 40)

**INTERNAL NOISE.** A form of mind cluttering that occurs when a person continually gives oneself negative messages that significantly affect TFA on both conscious and unconscious levels. With conscious internal noise, the person is aware of obsessive worrying, chronic anger, unresolved guilt, torturous regrets, deep sorrows, and unrelenting sadness. Unconscious internal noise is akin to free-floating anxiety, malaise, or merely feeling on edge. (pp. 71-72)

**INTERNAL THOUGHTS.** Inner words, ideas, and images that can sometimes trigger the same emotional response as an environmental press. (p. 37)

**INTERPERSONAL AWARENESS.** A firm grasp of relationships and group interactions. (p. 194)

**INTERPERSONAL CONNECTION.** Relationships reflecting an understanding and rapport between people. (p. 194)

**INTERPERSONAL IDENTITY (II).** The way a person comes to see and ultimately defines oneself through one-on-one contacts, associations, and relationships when the specific characteristics of the exchanges are consciously and unconsciously absorbed. (pp. 5, 87-88, 152, 234, & 243)

**INTERPERSONAL RELATIONSHIPS.** Contact through a variety of interactions, involving people, communities, and institutions. (p. 133)

**INTERPERSONAL SKILLS.** Expertise in negotiations and compromise affecting one's ability to develop trusting relationships. (pp. 29 & 116)

**INTIMIDATION.** A confrontation with someone or something deemed powerful and forbidding, causing one to surrender beliefs and principles. (p. 218)

**INTROSPECTION.** Self-reflecting that leads to understanding contradictions and confusions in one's personality that may be narrowing one's views. (p. 72)

**INTUITION.** An impression or sense about PSC. (pp. 16, 163, & 190)

**IQ/INTELLIGENCE QUOTIENT.** A traditional measurement of intelligence consisting of problem-solving, vocabulary, remembering facts, calculating, reasoning, and other basic cognitive functions. (p. 190)

**JUDGMENT.** Commonsense in understanding, drawing conclusions, and making decisions. (p. 116)

**JUDICIOUSNESS.** Making every effort to avoid exposing oneself to PSC in a way that may prove troublesome. (p. 126)

**KNOWLEDGE.** The processing of information through its acquisition, organization, conceptualization, and storage. (pp. 174 & 200)

**KNOWLEDGE ACQUIRED IN THE DEVELOPMENT OF PI.** Striving to understand world affairs. (p. 82)

**LEARNING DYSFUNCTIONS.** Neurological and neuropsychological disorders, including learning disabilities, attention deficit disorders (ADD), and attention-deficit hyperactivity disorder (ADHD), affecting concentration and impacting all cognitive functioning. (p. 58)

**LEARNINGS.** Understandings acquired through life experiences, academic institutions, informal settings, and the mentoring process. (pp. 174 & 228)

**LISTENING.** To put aside distractions, preoccupations, worries, and disappointments and attune to the subtleties of PSC. (p. 31)

**LOGICAL THOUGHT.** To reason and use dispassionate analysis. Unlike emotionalism, logical thought involves abstraction and conceptualization, synthesis of materials, and problem-solving. (p. 161)

**LONG-TERM MEMORY.** Recalling information after a significant amount of time has passed. (p. 160)

**LOW FRUSTRATION TOLERANCE.** Diminished patience due to delays or complexities in dealing with PSC. (pp. 172 & 227)

**MALEVOLENT IDENTIFICATIONS.** Powerful and intense connections to a person, institution, or idea leading to unprincipled, inhumane, or maladaptive TFA. (pp. 6, 110-111, & 244-245)

**MALICIOUS INTENT.** Spiteful ACR that are deliberate and calculated, often motivated by revenge. (p. 226)

**MANIPULATION AND EXPLOITATION** (see **EXPLOITATION**).

**MATERIALISM.** Highly valuing ownership of physical objects, with a need to purchase and possess an ever-increasing amount of "stuff." (p. 127)

**MATURITY.** Finding ways to maneuver through the developmental stages with adaptation, imagination, and perhaps inspiration in facing life's challenges. (pp. 29, 82, 208, 233-234, & 249)

**MEDIA MANIA.** The desire to obsessively follow the news via print, TV, or electronic devices, often involving watching violence, protests, and uprisings. (p. 134)

**MEMORY.** The ability to retain information, including short-term and long-term, systematic and rote, verbal-rote and verbal-conceptual, visual-spatial, and personal remembrances. (pp. 160-161)

**MENTAL DRIVE.** The degree to which a person's thinking is energetic and alert, thereby impacting the desire to learn and explore new avenues of thought. (p. 159-160)

**THE MENTORING PROCESS.** Direct learning through face-to-face interactions and affiliations. (p. 174)

**MICROMANAGING.** Excessive control and obsessive-compulsive approaches to problem-solving, resulting in stress for all concerned, especially in a work environment. (p. 192)

**MIND CLUTTERING.** Bogged down with a multitude of thoughts, regrets, and concerns, the most common feelings being of failure, guilt, regret, disappointment, grieving, discouragement, rumination, and vindictiveness. (pp. 38-40 & 71)

**MORALITY/MORAL REASONING.** A person's sense of right and wrong, usually developing over time but can occur suddenly through an epiphany. (pp. 82, 128, & 140)

**MOSAIC OF THE QUALITIES OF A VALUE SYSTEM.** The many characteristics of a person's wants and needs, forming distinctive patterns, with each value having opposing features. (p. 123)

**MOTIVATIONAL MISHAP.** A careless and hastily made decision based on intellectual miscalculation or emotional dysfunction. (p. 202)

**MULTIDIMENSIONAL THOUGHT.** To be able to hold multiple beliefs and ideas in one's mind and switch from one cognitive set to another. (pp. 164-165)

**NATURAL INSTINCTS APPROACH.** To look at things without preconceived notions of what is to come next; an impromptu, lets-not-get-too-ahead-of-ourselves approach. (p. 30)

**NEEDS.** Physiological, psychological, and acquired drives. (pp. 14-15)

**NEGATIVITY.** Continually finding fault with oneself, others, situations, or circumstances. It is adversarial, pessimistic, cynical, and complaining. (pp. 52 & 89-90)

**NEUROLOGICAL AND NEUROPSYCHOLOGICAL DYS-FUNCTIONS** (see **LEARNING DYSFUNCTIONS**). Various brain disorders that impair concentration and other cognitive function-ing. (p. 58)

**NEXIS POINTS.** The focal points that bind concepts together. (pp.

41 & 165)

**NON-CONFORMING AND REBELLIOUS** (see **REBELLION**). Doing one's "own thing" and going against the grain, being obstinate and resistant to change. (p. 29)

**OBJECTIFICATION OR REALISM.** The act of making PSC quantifiable, observable, external, embodied, and concrete. (pp. 82-83 & 161)

**OBJECTIVITY.** A dispassionate and unbiased view of PSC. (pp. 28, 82, 138, & 163)

**OBSESSIONS.** Recurrent, repetitive thoughts, ideas, and themes that either involve avoiding what is feared or seeking what is wanted. (pp. 39 & 143-144)

**OBSESSIVE-COMPULSIVE TENDENCIES.** Hypercritical and judgmental, with a need for order and control. (p. 193)

**OPENNESS.** A willingness to be objective, flexible, and optimistic. (pp. 163-164)

**OPTIMAL THINKING** (see **UNCONSCIOUS, TYPES 3 AND 6**). Processing information and making decisions expediently and efficiently, utilizing focused attention, logic, objectification, coherence, organization, vision, simplification, and reconciliation of thought. (pp. 177-181 & 247)

**OPTIMISM.** Seeing the positive possibilities. (pp. 37, 164, & 175)

**ORGANIZATION.** The systematic and methodical arranging of ideas and reasonings that generally require careful planning and preparation, self-discipline and self-control, and strategizing. (p. 162)

**ORGANIZATIONAL APPROACH.** A step-by-step, procedural approach to problem-solving using anticipation, planning, and developing strategies and fallbacks. (p. 30)

**OUTLIER PC** (see **TRIGGERS**). PCs that stand out because they are significantly at odds with other PCs. Usually unconscious, it is a "stand-alone," the product of a particular identification process, often involving trauma and forming early in life. (pp. 211-212, 235-236, & 247-248)

**OVERCOMPENSATION** (see **EXTRAORDINARY COMPENSATION**). Taking extreme measures to overcome a weakness or flaw in one's TFA. (pp. 112 & 141)

**OVERCONTROLLING, OBSESSIVE, PERFECTIONISTIC.** Emphasizing rules and procedures and giving unimportant details weight, while missing relevant information and issues. Insecurity is present, causing rigidity, stubbornness, and intolerance; cooperation and compromise are minimal. (p. 29)

**OVER-PLANNING.** Extreme preparation that compromises sharpness as the individual becomes unimaginative, rigidly adhering to a preset plan. (p. 192)

**OVER-REACTIVITY.** Emotional responses expressed or held inside that are unrealistic and inappropriate, leading to instability. (p. 172)

**PANIC.** A state of alarm and trepidation. (p. 193)

**PASSION.** A strong emotion that may help or hurt one's prospects for success, usually involving high energy, enthusiasm, intense drive, fierce devotion, and deep-rooted commitment. Examples include involvement in a relationship, commitment to a cause, dedication to an institution, and engagement in studies. (pp. 53, 73-74, & 135-136)

**PASSIVE-AGGRESSIVE.** Showing resentment and hostility indirectly and finding a way to blame others for problems. (p. 29)

**PAST, PRESENT, AND FUTURE.** A perspective on the role of time frames in understanding issues and making decisions. Awareness of the past, attunement to the present, and preparation for the future are essential in reducing the occurrence and impact of ACR. (pp. 41-42 & 229-230)

**PATHOS** (see **UNCONSCIOUS, TYPE 1**). An aggregate of emotionally charged aspects of a person, including unresolved conflicts, traumas, and malevolent identifications, as well as emotionalism that causes an expansion of adverse and destructive images toward oneself and others. It is primarily an outgrowth of personal identity (PI), gradually pulling away as it becomes an independent function of the personality. (pp. 6, 107-108, 153, 170, 181, 227, 234, & 243)

**PATIENCE.** Taking whatever time is necessary to determine what is worthwhile, insignificant, or simply wrong. (pp. 73 & 173-174)

**PEACE AND COMPLACENCY AS VALUES.** Seeking an agreeable and accommodating life that offers tranquility and harmony. (p. 126)

**PEOPLE.** Interpersonal influences, a primary factor in human identifications, strongly impacting one's TFA. (p. 25)

**PEOPLE, SITUATIONS, AND CIRCUMSTANCES (PSC)** (see **ENVIRONMENTAL PRESS**). The particular set of conditions to which one is exposed. (pp. 25-26, 83-84, 122, & 208)

**PERCEPTION.** The ability to form impressions of PSC accurately with an in-depth understanding of conscious and unconscious motivations. (pp. 82, 90, 120, 164, & 185)

**PERFECTIONISM.** Devotion to making no mistakes with an

over-control of PSC and heavy-handed criticism of oneself and others. (pp. 113 & 140-141)

**PERSEVERATION.** Recycling and repetition of TFA. (pp. 40-41)

**PERSONA.** The image a person displays to the outside world, which may or may not be significantly different from inner thoughts and feelings. (pp. 51 & 122)

**PERSONAL IDENTITY (PI).** The sense of who a person is, the individual traits to which one relates. It is how a person defines oneself, including qualities and characteristics and peculiarities—the good, the bad, and the ugly—that distinguish one person from another in TFA. (pp. 5, 19, 79-80, 152, 233-234, & 243)

**PERSONALITY CONSTRUCTS.** An army of little personalities created by the identification process that may work with or against each other. (pp. 207-209 & 247-248)

**PERSONALITY ELEMENTS** (same as **ELEMENTS OF PERSONALITY**).

**PERSONAL MEMORIES.** Recalling friendships, family relationships, successes and failures, and other past events and experiences. (p. 161)

**PERSPECTIVES.** A person's overarching view, reflecting the elements of personality, whether or not they are integrated and balanced. (pp. 36-37, 123, & 229)

**PESSIMISM.** A general outlook that is cynical and distrustful, viewing life through a "lens of negativity." (pp. 37, 39, 108, & 175)

**PHYSIOLOGICAL NEEDS.** Biological requirements to sustain life and physically survive, including food, water, air, shelter, and climatic conditions. (p. 14)

**PHYSIOLOGICAL REACTIONS/PHYSIOLOGY**. Muscle tension, aches, pains, and generalized bodily-based symptoms caused by stress. (pp. 69-70)

**PLAYING IT SAFE**. The goal is to conserve and keep one's status and possessions. (pp. 126-127)

**POINT OF VIEW**. Establishing criteria for a value. (p. 123)

**POLITICAL AND MANIPULATIVE, DECEPTIVE, CONTROLLING, CALCULATING, AND SCHEMING**. Lacking integrity and utilizing underhanded tactics to exploit others. (p. 29)

**POST TRAUMATIC STRESS DISORDER (PTSD)**. The most widely known effect of trauma that may include flashbacks, in which a person reexperiences the event. Suddenly, typically laced with fear, overwhelming anxiety, and panic, the trauma is back in full force and can be debilitating, catastrophic, and emotionally exhausting. Recovery from such events is typically partial, fragmented, and uneven, reappearing when triggered by an image, thought, memory, or encounter. (p. 54)

**POWER AND CONTROL**. An overriding desire to exercise authority over others by whatever means necessary. (pp. 110 & 127)

**PRACTICAL REASONING**. A way of thinking that allows one to stay grounded by not losing sight of the basics. In other words, to "get real" and recognize the most critical issues in everyday functioning by using common sense and pragmatism. (p. 161)

**PRAGMATISM**. Keeping things simple and responding to the obvious needs of a problem. (pp. 83, 127, & 162)

**PREPARATION.** Developing steadfastness, drive, and energy to learn something well and master it. (p. 173)

**THE PRIMA DONNA COMPLEX.** An obsession with one's own needs and desires, often coming from having been overindulged during childhood and treated as if one can do no wrong. (pp. 112 & 135)

**PROBLEMATIC IDENTITY.** A person develops a disjointed and fragmented PI, leading to an expansion of pathos. (p. 135)

**PROBLEMATIC UNCONSCIOUS INFLUENCES.** Continuing to utilize unsuccessful and perhaps destructive approaches in dealing with people, situations, and circumstances (PSC) that are outside of one's awareness. (pp. 40-41)

**PROBLEM-SOLVING.** The careful study of variables, including those that are not obviously connected, requiring initial theorizing about these factors and ruling out alternative explanations. (pp. 161, 167, & 173)

**PROCESS OF THOUGHT.** A person is alert and conscious of one's world, accurately perceiving what is there and comprehending its meaning and significance. (p. 7)

**PROCRASTINATION.** An inability to get things done decisively, quickly, and without hesitation. (p. 116)

**PROPORTIONALITY.** A sense of harmony in the value system. (pp. 121-122)

**PSEUDO-EMOTIONS.** The result of virtual reality becoming an integral part of daily life with an indulgence in pastimes that involve flights of imagination, having some of the characteristics of emotional reactions, traits, states, flow, and remembrances but in which the feelings have no depth or a visceral history attached to them. (pp. 49-50)

**PSYCHOLOGICAL NEEDS**. The contact with people and other life forms, and intellectual and physical stimulation that are essential for human functioning. (p. 14)

**PSYCHOSOMATIC REACTIONS**. Physical symptoms that are a result of an unresolved emotional issue with underlying forces originating in the psyche. (p. 70)

**PSYKHE**. In Greek mythology, the goddess of the soul, spirit, and mind. The word psyche refers to this same essence: the totality of consciousness and unconsciousness. (p. 3)

**RADICAL RENEWAL**. When adopting new values requires a complete reorganization of beliefs. (p. 123)

**RATIONALIZATION** (see **EDITING OF TFA**). A form of editing that involves avoiding taking responsibility for one's actions by justifying, exaggerating, or minimizing one's role. (p. 133)

**RAW EMOTIONS**. An entirely visceral expression of one's feelings, with little or no cognitive component. (p. 20)

**REALITY TESTING**. PI expands with the development of objectivity, grounding, pragmatism, and experiential learning. (pp. 82-83, 120-121, 135, 172, 193-194, & 202)

**REBELLION** (see **NON-CONFORMING** and **REBELLIOUS**). The opposition to societal standards. (pp. 29, 52, 80, & 201)

**RECOGNIZING REALITY**. Acknowledging and objectifying one's TFA in response to PSC. (p. 172)

**RECOGNIZING THE PAIN**. Acknowledging the emotional distress and discomfort of an upsetting event. (p. 238)

**REGRESSIONS**. Psychologically functioning at one level of development and then backsliding to an earlier stage to temporarily reduce emotional discomfort. (pp. 236-238)

**REGRET BASED ON LOST OPPORTUNITY**. Continuously thinking about "what could have been" if only one had followed through when one had the chance. (p. 39)

**RIGIDITY**. An unwillingness to be open and flexible in TFA. (pp. 116 & 194)

**RELATIVITY**. The belief that values are completely fluid, interchangeable, and without definition. (p. 128)

**RELIGIOSITY**. The practice of one's faith, including institutional membership, practiced in a formal setting, with specific doctrines and dogmas, Scriptures, inspired books, and other sacred writings. (p. 129)

**RISK-TAKING**. Actions that may be impulsive and reckless, possibly exposing a person to significant danger. (pp. 134, 167, & 216)

**ROTE MEMORY**. Recalling materials with no logical connections, like a series of numbers. (p. 160)

**RUMINATING**. A thought process that involves chronic worrying or concern, obsessing over anything and everything. (p. 39)

**SELF DECEPTION**. The censoring and editing of TFA. (p. 220)

**SELF-DESTRUCTIVENESS**. When a person lacks survival and self-preservation instincts, with a decline in watchfulness, self-care, caution, and practicality. (p. 140)

**SELF INDULGENCE.** Engaging in pleasures and curiosities with little concern for others. (pp. 138-139)

**SELFISHNESS.** Narcissistic self-indulgence, with a lack of empathy, concern, and care for others. (p. 193)

**SELF-OBSESSED.** When a person is overly concerned with oneself, including possessions and appearance, with the entire focus being "what's in it for me." (pp. 112 & 126)

**SEMICONSCIOUS STATES.** Not fully awake and alert to internal thoughts and feelings or external actions and events. Perception, recognition, and understanding are not completely engaged; thought processes lack consistency and constancy. (pp. 58-59)

**SENSATION-SEEKING.** One makes choices based on a desire to experience intense stimulation. (p. 216)

**SENSITIVITIES AND VULNERABILITIES.** The subtleties of nonverbal interpersonal contact—body language, tone and volume of voice, facial expressions, hesitations and pauses, interruptions, firmness in the way one speaks, and movements of the hands and arms—play a role in experiences and intensify in face-to-face inter-actions. (pp. 22, 109, 170-171, 211-212, 235-236, & 248-249)

**SENSITIZED TO NUANCES.** Grasping PSC's distinctive and id-iosyncratic elements in determining which responses will be most effective at any moment in time. (p. 191)

**SHARPNESS.** The ability to have acute, farsighted, penetrating, crafty, calculating, and perceptive insights; seeing the significance of a person, situation, or circumstance (PSC), the motivations, intrica-cies, and vulnerabilities. A form of intelligence that allows one to see the significance of complex and confounding PSC. (pp. 189-190 & 247)

**SHEER NUMBER OF PCs.** PCs proliferate with the possibility of more separations in the personality. (p. 210)

**SHORT-TERM MEMORY.** Holding knowledge for a brief amount of time. (p. 160)

**SIMPLIFICATION.** To cut out redundancy, confusion, and unnecessary complications in the following ways: spelling out details, making things plain, and reducing information overload. (pp. 162-163)

**SITUATIONS.** A somewhat predictable and planned set of events in which there is typically an opportunity for the person to prepare a response. (pp. 25-26)

**SKEPTICISM AS AN EXPRESSION OF EMOTIONALISM.** Doubt, questioning, and disbelief within a rigid and controlling personality, imprisoned with endless procedures, rules, and regulations. (pp. 115-116)

**SOCIAL AWARENESS AND SOCIAL INTELLIGENCE.** The ability to keenly observe the dynamics between and among people in assessing PSC with a critical understanding of the conscious and unconscious motivating forces behind persons and institutions. (p. 164)

**SOCIAL INHIBITIONS.** Difficulty being assertive and forthcoming. (p. 193)

**SOCIALLY UNSKILLED.** Acting inappropriately with deficiencies in interpersonal abilities. (p. 29)

**SOCIAL WITHDRAWAL.** Pulling away from problematic PSC,

even when issues urgently need to be faced. (p. 219)

**SOCIETAL STANDARDS ACQUIRED IN THE DEVELOP-MENT OF II**. A recognition of the mores of society. (p. 90)

**SOMETHING OF SIGNIFICANCE.** That which matters to a person enough to know when to set aside a balanced approach to take action outside the norm due to a crisis. It will vary from person to person, situation to situation, and circumstance to circumstance. (p. 139)

**SPIRITUALITY**. Although identification with humanity, nature or even the universe may be present, the focus is on the intangible and the invisible, with a de-emphasis on the buildings and rituals of conventional religion. (p. 129)

**SPIRITUS** (see **UNCONSCIOUS, TYPE 9**). One's innate, innermost character and disposition, including qualities there from the beginning that are not the product of learning and do not change with time or life experiences. (pp. 7, 66, 149-150, 182, 208, 234, & 246)

**STABILITY OF PCs**. Since the connections among PCs are continually changing, they will react against one another, and their relationships will lack stability. (p. 209)

**STANDARDS**. Judging and appraising a person, object, or idea to determine if they are at a certain level, based on set criteria, as in assessing aesthetics or truth-telling. (pp. 129-133)

**STATES**. Temporary conditions that affect a person's perception and TFA, with common ones being sleep deprivation, alcohol intoxication, drug ingestion, acute or long-standing health problems, or a brief but intense emotional reaction that can energize or deplete a person. (p. 36)

**STAYING ON TRACK**. To remain focused on the task at hand and not allow extraneous TFA to take root. (p. 31)

**STEADFAST IN APPROACH**. Managing daily obligations and duties. (p. 174)

**STRATEGIC PHILOSOPHY (SP)**. A personal belief system, operating on conscious and unconscious levels, the aim of which is to predict how people and institutions will act and react across the spectrum of situations and circumstances (PSC). (pp. 197-198 & 247)

**STREET SMARTS**. The ability to interpret PSC accurately, especially reading others' subtle intentions. (p. 37)

**STRENGTH OF PCs**. The characteristics of the initial identifications and subsequent reinforcements determine PCs' power. (p. 210)

**STRESS**. Life experiences that disrupt TFA, including fatigue, discomfort and pain, noise and distracting sounds, unpleasant PSC, job pressures, financial difficulties, sleep deprivation, and poor health. (pp. 53-54, 170, 182-183, & 237)

**STRIVING TOWARD CLEARMIND** (see **CLEARMIND**).

**STYLE**. The manner and aura of a person's actions, distinguishing one person from another by their visual qualities. (pp. 22 & 80)

**SUSPICIOUS AND UNTRUSTWORTHY**. Reluctant to take PSC at face value, one looks for hidden meanings and motives in others' behaviors. (p. 112)

**SUSTAINED ATTENTION**. Continued focus on the subject matter at hand. (p. 160)

**SYNTHESIS OF MATERIALS.** An in-depth review and blending of issues to make the necessary connections, combining concepts and information into coherent wholes. (pp. 82 & 161)

**SYSTEMATIC MEMORY.** Recall based on logical or organized associations. (p. 160)

**TEMPERAMENTAL REACTIONS.** Fleeting emotions merely passing through that exaggerate a person's responses and are frequently associated with anger, outbursts, and even rage. (p. 208)

**THOUGHT-EMOTION CONNECTIONS.** When thoughts influence emotions and emotions influence thoughts instantaneously and automatically. (pp. 37-38)

**THOUGHTS.** A conglomerate of cognitions, impressions, and the belief system a person has adopted. (p. 35)

**THRILL.** A desire to be part of an exciting adventure. (p. 111)

**TIME.** As a person ages, PI changes which may signify personal growth or instability. (p. 84)

**TIME MANAGEMENT.** Spending an appropriate amount of time and energy on materials. (p. 173)

**TIME'S EFFECT ON PI DEVELOPMENT.** Some people continually adjust, adapt, and modify PI, while others tend to stay about the same throughout their lifetime. (p. 84)

**TOUGHNESS OF SPIRIT.** The emotional qualities required to handle especially difficult PSC effectively. (pp. 109-110)

**TRAITS.** The repetition of a particular set of thoughts, feelings, or actions. (pp. 35-36 & 178)

**TRANSFORMING THE EVENT.** Reorder, rearrange, and reconfigure the TFA that affects one's identity. (p. 238)

**TRANSPERSONAL IDENTITY (TI).** A person's identification with a non-material reality, typically involving an intrapsychic connection with God, the cosmos, or other spiritual domain, none of which can be directly known and primarily resting on faith and intuition. (pp. 5-6, 101-102, 153, 234, & 243)

**TRAUMAS/TRAUMATIC EXPERIENCES** (see **POST TRAUMATIC STRESS DISORDER**). Distressing and disturbing experiences commonly resulting from physical assaults that may debilitate and emotionally exhaust a person, and may continue to cause psychological dysfunction years later. (pp. 6, 54, 109-110, 236-237, & 243)

**TRIGGERS** (see **OUTLIER PC**). Individualized emotional sensitivities, usually unconscious and the result of a conditioning process that cause an exaggerated response in which a rapid and radical change in mood, temperament, and personality are set in motion. (pp. 22, 211-212, & 248)

**TRUTH-TELLING.** Seeking out objective standards in appraising knowledge, utilizing logic, reason, scientific study, impartial findings, detailed inquiry, and analysis. (pp. 130-133)

**TWISTING OF THE FACTS.** Distorting what is known to be accurate while retaining some elements of the truth, including willful contortions designed to discredit a person, position, institution, or idea. (p. 185)

**UNCONSCIOUS STATES** (see **UNCONSCIOUS, TYPES 1-9**). One is unaware of TFA; ideas and images are uncertain and out of focus. (pp. 16, 41-42, 59-61, 120, & 198-199)

**UNCONSCIOUS TYPE 1: THE BLOCKING OF COGNI-TIVE-EMOTIONAL CONNECTIONS** (see **PATHOS**). An inability to remember something unpleasant that has happened. In tandem with pathos, this lack of recall operates unconsciously throughout the entire personality and is especially dominant in directives. As pathos evolves, so does the blocking of cognitive-emotional connections; they align, complement, and connect. A symbolic-psychological-emotional undercurrent is operating. (pp. 60-61)

**UNCONSCIOUS, TYPE 2: THE INTEGRATION OF COGNI-TIVE-EMOTIONAL CONNECTIONS.** A process of internal healing, with the emotional turmoil of CTMI at least partially resolved on an unconscious level. Opposing and contrasting elements of the psyche consolidate through integration and synthesis; a person's inner character and inherent emotional strengths are the catalysts for these changes. A symbolic-psychological-emotional undercurrent is present. (p. 61)

**UNCONSCIOUS, TYPE 3: ADAPTATION AND ADJUSTMENT OF COGNITIONS.** When the mind is able to integrate one's knowledge and experiences without deliberate or focused thought processes, absorbing and incorporating information already stored, modifying and transforming one's understandings. No symbolic-psychological-emotional component is present. (pp. 61-62)

**UNCONSCIOUS, TYPE 4: ASSOCIATIONS FORMED THROUGH THE INTENTIONAL OR ACCIDENTAL PAIRING OF TFA.** Connections created through classical conditioning, formed by simple associations. Thinking may be minimal, with connections formed only by the pairing of stimuli and responses, unrelated to a reinforcement. No symbolic-psychological-emotional undercurrent involved in the process. (pp. 62-63)

**UNCONSCIOUS, TYPE 5: ASSOCIATIONS FORMED THROUGH INTENTIONAL OR ACCIDENTAL REWARDING**

**OR PUNISHING OF TFA.** When the person's TFA are reinforced—via a "reward" or a "punishment"—based on his response (R-1) to a particular stimulus (S-1). If exposed to a different stimulus (S-2), there is no such reinforcer to the person's response (R-1). Similarly, if exposed to that original stimulus (S-1) and a person responds in another way (R-2), again, no reinforcer will be forthcoming. Thinking may be minimal, with connections formed only through the pairing of stimuli and reinforcement of the response which has become almost automatic. The associations determine the response, with no symbolic-psychological-emotional undercurrent playing a significant role. (pp. 63-64)

**UNCONSCIOUS, TYPE 6: CONNECTIONS FORMED THROUGH INTENTIONAL OR ACCIDENTAL LEARNINGS** (see **AUTOMATIONS**). Knowledge and skills acquired through continual adjustments and adaptations. Learnings may become automations, activities with no motivational significance attached to those unconscious TFA. No symbolic-psychological-emotional undercurrent is present. (p. 64)

**UNCONSCIOUS, TYPE 7: THE EXPRESSION OF INSTINCTUAL URGES**. TFA involving sexual attractions, empathetic concerns, aggressive actions, and other biological urges. A person may simply respond to the urge without thinking processes being a significant factor. No symbolic-psychological-emotional undercurrent is present. (p. 65)

**UNCONSCIOUS, TYPE 8: DREAM STATES AND THE EXPRESSION OF IMAGINAL CONNECTIONS**. As a person sleeps, expresses thoughts and feelings, whether or not the messages are consciously received or understood. A symbolic-psychological-emotional undercurrent may or may not be present. (pp. 65-66)

**UNCONSCIOUS, TYPE 9: THE INNATE AND NATURAL EXPRESSION OF SPIRITUS.** Going about the routines of daily life without paying attention to one's essential nature. No symbolic-psychological-emotional undercurrent is present. (p. 66)

**UNDERSTANDING**. Being savvy, smart, and possibly shrewd in dealing with ideas, people, and institutions. (pp. 184-185)

**UNINFORMED**. Relying on inaccurate and unreliable information. (pp. 193-194)

**UNIQUENESS OF PCs**. PCs will not necessarily have all elements of the personality, and some may have only a single element. (p. 210)

**UNRESOLVED CTMI**. Deep-seated insecurities that continue to interfere with all elements of the personality and distort the development of a person's strategic philosophy. (pp. 202 & 236)

**VALUE CLARIFICATION**. Detailing one's wants and needs and coming to terms with contradictions and inconsistencies in one's life and lifestyle. (pp. 121-124)

**VICARIOUS LIVING AND SPECTATOR SPORTS**. Experiences through observing others, which can serve as a distraction from the stresses of modern life but also become an obsession. (pp. 133-134)

**VINDICATIVE**. When a person believes one "has been wronged" and obsesses on getting even. (pp. 39-40)

**VISION** (see **HOLISM**).

**VISUAL-SPATIAL MEMORY**. The ability to recall shapes, sizes, angles, locations, and movements. (p. 160)

**VULNERABILITIES** (see **SENSITIVITIES AND VULNERABILITIES**).

**WANTS.** Desires ranging from mild attractions to full-blown cravings that can expand and evolve into compulsions that cause extreme behaviors. (p. 15)

**WARMTH.** An emotional state that radiates friendliness, closeness, and familiarity. (p. 12)

**WEIGHTING AND RANKING OF VALUES.** A person's ratings of wants and needs, reflecting their importance and significance. (p. 122)

**WILLINGNESS TO ACT.** When a person's values require one to take steps that involve risking reputation, career, or lifestyle. (p. 122)

**WITHDRAWAL** (see **CENSORING OF TFA**). A form of censoring that involves becoming socially inhibited, primarily due to generalized anxiety. (p. 132)

# ABOUT THE AUTHOR

MARIANO GALLO's professional background has involved clinical, consulting, teaching, research, and supervisory work. After completing a clinical residency and dissertation study at Northwestern University Medical School, he received a Ph.D. in clinical psychology from Miami University (Ohio). He previously obtained an M.A. degree in clinical psychology from Roosevelt University and a B.S. degree in psychology from Loyola University. He is a past fellow of the National Institute of Mental Health (NIMH) and a life member of the American Psychological Association (APA). His primary focus is on the psychology of personality. He is a co-founder of Consultants in Applied Psychology (CAP) and a licensed clinical psychologist in Illinois (active) and California (inactive). Get in touch with Mariano at consultantsinappliedpsychology@gmail.com.